THE
SECRETS
TO
DELIVERANCE

ALEXANDER PAGANI

CHARISMA
HOUSE

THE SECRETS TO DELIVERANCE
by Alexander Pagani
Published by Charisma House
Charisma Media/Charisma House Book Group
600 Rinehart Road
Lake Mary, Florida 32746
www.charismahouse.com

Cover design by Vincent Pirozzi
Design Director: Justin Evans

Visit the author's website at www.alexanderpagani.com.

Library of Congress Cataloging-in-Publication Data

Names: Pagani, Alexander, author.
Title: The secrets to deliverance / Alexander Pagani.
Description: Lake Mary, Florida : Charisma House, 2018. | Includes
    bibliographical references and index.
Identifiers: LCCN 2018011642 (print) | LCCN 2018021486 (ebook) | ISBN
    9781629995144 | ISBN 9781629995137 (trade paper : alk. paper)
Subjects: LCSH: Spiritual warfare. | Exorcism. | Demonology.
Classification: LCC BV4509.5 (ebook) | LCC BV4509.5 .P328 2018 (print) | DDC
    235/.4--dc23
LC record available at https://lccn.loc.gov/2018011642
International Standard Book Number: 978-1-62999-513-7
E-book ISBN: 978-1-62999-514-4

23 24 25 26 27 — 17 16 15 14 13
Printed in the United States of America

CONTENTS

ACKNOWLEDGMENTS

To the Holy Spirit, thank You for granting me wisdom and insight into the mysteries of the kingdom and entrusting me with the secrets to deliverance to continue Your work of setting the captive free. To my Lord and Savior, Jesus Christ, thank You for choosing me and entrusting me with this ministry. To my heavenly Father, I'm eternally grateful to You for giving my life purpose and meaning. You're worthy to receive all glory, honor, majesty, and power!

To my loving wife and best friend, Ibelize Pagani, thank you for believing in me from day one. I'm still desperately in love with you after all these years. You're the most amazing woman I've ever met. Words can't express how grateful I am for the countless times you saved our ministry with your ability to hear God in your dreams. You're my personal prophet, and I love you with all my heart!

To my sons, Apollos and Xavier, I love you both. Thank you for completely understanding God's call on my life and sharing me with the world without resentment. To see you both loving God and growing up into men who love God with all your hearts is what I live for! Dad is so proud of you both.

To my parents, Nancy and Alexander Pagani; my grandmother, Emilia Rivera; my aunts Vilma Batista and Marilyn Rivera; and all my cousins and immediate family who have been there for me my whole life, thank you for your loving support throughout the years, especially during the darkest moments of my life. I love and appreciate every one of you. I'm blessed to be part of our family. And to my in-laws, Bienvenido and Sarah Montes, I love you and thank you for all your support!

To the greatest church, He Is Risen Tabernacle (HIRT), where would I be without you? Words can't express how much I love all of you. We've been on an amazing journey together all these years, and we're leaving a legacy for future generations. I'm honored to be called your pastor and to lead such an *amazing church*.

Finally this book is dedicated to all the deliverance ministers who pioneered a path for future generations to follow: Win Worley, Derek Prince, John Eckhardt, Frank Hammond, Ivory Hopkins, Don Basham, Neil T. Anderson, H. A. Maxwell Whyte, Kimberly Daniels, Ana Mendez Ferrell, Guillermo Maldonado, as well as all the Catholic exorcists and every other deliverance minister who remains unnamed and hidden behind the scenes, setting the captive free at no charge. I honor you all, and I'm humbled to be counted among you.

INTRODUCTION

ALEX, WHAT ARE you doing? You're embarrassing your-self in front of the core leadership." That's what I was thinking as I felt myself being pinned to the floor by an unseen supernatural force. I was a pastor who'd helped dozens of people get free of demonic oppression. But a church business meeting took an unusual turn, and I found myself on the floor with what felt like a giant foot on my back and my ministry team taking authority over a demon that was manifesting.

As I wondered how in the world I'd ended up in such an embarrassing position, I heard a voice whisper in my ear, "I've been sent to remove this demon. I'm allowing it to manifest so I can remove it." Those words from the angel with its foot on my back helped me later. But at the time knowing God was allowing the situation didn't make it any easier to swallow. Because I couldn't control what was happening to me, rage and embarrassment filled every part of me. I squirmed on the floor, wanting to throw something but unable to really move because of that huge unseen foot on my back. Then suddenly a loud shriek came out of my mouth, and I heard my core ministry staff begin to take authority over the demon. Thankfully that was the beginning of the end.

Prior to the demonic manifestation, we were having a staff meeting, and some minor disagreements quickly escalated into an argument. I was angry over something that I knew was insignificant, but I couldn't control myself. I'd felt that anger before, and to be completely honest, I was tired of fighting it, so I took my glasses off and said, "I really need to get free from this." That is the last thing I remember before I woke up on the floor with the angel's foot on my back, wondering why I was embarrassing myself.

I spent about five minutes on the floor before I let out that loud shriek (which lasted for at least thirty seconds), and then the demon left. Immediately I heard the voice in my ear again, this time saying, "The demon of destruction is gone. Don't look for it." An overwhelming peace swept over me, and I noticed that my chest felt different. Even after I accepted Christ, I carried myself with a kind of bravado that I learned growing up in the Bronx. It wasn't just a way I walked or talked; I literally felt something in my chest. But now it was gone, and everyone who knew me could tell the difference.

I got saved in prison and learned deliverance because I and people I ministered to were dealing with issues that counseling and inner healing couldn't seem to solve. Through the years God had been showing me step by step how to help people get free. But my experience at our church that day convinced me that there was even more to deliverance than I realized. Christians could not only need deliverance, but demons could lodge themselves in hidden areas of our lives—both in our souls and in our body parts. I knew the demon that caused me to feel such rage was literally residing in my chest, because after I was set free I felt a physical difference.

I realized that if a demon could live in a body part, then I needed to look further into where else an unclean spirit might hide so that as a deliverance minister I could be more targeted and specific in my prayers. I began seeking God for answers, and a couple months later I had a dream. In it I was approached by a well-known ministry leader who told me to open my hand. When I did, this person gave me a little book with the title *The Secrets to Deliverance* shining in gold letters. The minister then closed my hands, and I woke up.

From that day until now, my spirit has been receiving download after download of insight into the realm of the human soul and the demonic. Shortly after that dream God began showing me why it can take so long for some people to get free, myself included. God revealed that the human soul can be shattered in pieces as Psalm 7:2 says, "Lest he tear my soul like a lion, rending it in pieces, while there is none to deliver" (KJV). Demons hide in these fragmented pieces in the human soul until someone cleans up the mess and picks up the pieces.

Each of these pieces represents a part of you, or a fragment of your personality. When I first received this revelation, I called these pieces "fragments," but as time progressed, I began seeing this revelation throughout Scripture, and I recognized these fragments as "rooms" in the soul. I began to teach the revelation God was giving me during our midweek Bible study, and there was an incredible response each time. The most hardened members of our church were being instantly set free as we began going into the rooms of their souls and removing the most hidden demons.

This book shares my experience along with proven biblical strategies for evicting demons hiding in body parts and cleaning out the rooms of the soul to bring people into deeper levels of deliverance. If you've ever prayed for someone and just couldn't seem to break through, or if you've sought deliverance for yourself again and again and nothing seems to change, this revelation is for you. God wants to upgrade your understanding of deliverance so you can finally experience breakthrough.

DELIVERANCE 2.0

The demons that lodge themselves in the rooms of our souls and in our body parts don't respond to cookie-cutter deliverance formulas. Getting rid of them requires targeted, specific prayer under the leading of the Holy Spirit. I've heard from many deliverance ministers who complain about encountering tough cases that seem to resist breakthrough. They're not having this difficulty because they aren't willing to roll up their sleeves and tarry with a person until he is set free. It's because many still view deliverance as being one-size-fits-all, and they don't realize all the places demons can hide in a person's life or how to specifically address those areas.

Deliverance is less like a maze that you can trace your steps to find your way out of and more like a labyrinth. In a labyrinth nothing is where it should be, and nothing is as it seems. It's a series of trap doors, backward stairs, and small doors, and what you thought was the exit actually places you right back at the beginning. Demons want you to keep applying certain strategies the church learned in the 1970s because they know you'll likely never find their hiding places using those approaches.

Many years ago I was in a very difficult situation, and I didn't know how to get out of it. During that time I had a dream in which I was facing a house, and sitting on the front steps was a bunch of young thugs who were making it difficult for me to enter the house. As I climbed over them, I ended up on the first floor of an apartment building. It was dark and gloomy. In the distance I saw a staircase and decided to take the steps leading upstairs. As I was walking up the steps, they seemed to be leading in many different directions. The steps finally led me to a room in the attic. When I opened the door, I saw a life-size mannequin sitting on the floor. As I approached the plastic mannequin, it woke up, terrified that it had been discovered. In fear it got up and ran out of the attic.

When I woke up from the dream, the Holy Spirit let me know that the situation I was facing wasn't a maze that I could find my way out of by simply backtracking. It was a labyrinth that had many trap doors, and I would need wisdom to problem solve and find my way out. This is around the time when the Lord began giving me the revelation of demons hiding in our rooms and body parts.

Every person is unique. To assume that a cookie-cutter approach to deliverance will produce the same results with every person is foolishness. While some principles can be applied to every deliverance session, God wants to give us the specific strategies each individual needs to experience freedom.

That is why I have written this book. The Holy Spirit desires that the church gain a deeper revelation about deliverance. Using ineffective weapons and tactics in deliverance ministry does not please the Holy Spirit. I'll even go so far as to say it is a form of idolatry because it prizes forms and rituals over the truth God wants to reveal. The Spirit of the Lord wants to release fresh insight, new strategies, and new weapons. He longs to take us deep and show us exactly where demons hide and how to expel them. He wants to upgrade our model for deliverance to one that is fresh, tactical, and effective. This is the inheritance of the saints: "To bind their kings with chains, and their nobles with fetters of iron" (Ps. 149:8, KJV).

ARE DEMONS BEHIND EVERYTHING?

Jesus died so we could live in total freedom (Gal. 5:1), but so many people are not living in that reality. I wrote this book for those dealing with stubborn issues that they just can't seem to overcome. Counseling hasn't worked. Inner healing has helped some, but the problem persists, which is what was happening with me. This is not to say every issue a person faces has a demon at its root. Sometimes a person needs to be transformed by the renewing of his mind as Romans 12:2 says. But when you've done everything you know to do to overcome a persistent problem and still there's no breakthrough, you're more than likely dealing with a demon.

As you're reading this book, you may begin to think, "There seems to be way too much emphasis on the devil and demons." But I assure you, that is not the case. The devil's number one form of deception is to make the world believe he doesn't exist, and his number two form of deception is to make the church believe we blame him too much. Modern evangelical ministers don't blame the devil enough because they're too occupied saying things such as, "It's not the devil—it's you!" For some people that is the case, but there are times when the problem is 100 percent demonic and must be confronted as such! The average believer hears about Satan and the works of darkness only once a year during the annual spiritual warfare conference or when calamity strikes within the church and the congregation is forced to look more closely at the demonic. This book is designed to keep the demonic fresh in your worldview so you won't be ignorant of Satan's devices (2 Cor. 2:11).

As you might have guessed, I believe Christians can be oppressed by demons. When we accept Christ, we belong to God, but we can allow demonic spirits to gain a foothold in areas of our lives we haven't surrendered to the Lord. I will explain this further in chapter 2, but for now I'll just say that demons cannot possess a believer, but they can wreak havoc in the areas of a Christian's life to which they have been given access.

But there is good news. Through the revelation in this book I have seen even those with the toughest cases of demonic bondage set free by the power of God. The authority we have been given through Christ is irresistible, and once you know where demons like to hide and how to remove them, they will have no choice but to leave.

This journey will take you deep, but in the end you will have a clear understanding of how demons enter the rooms of our temples and our body parts. We will begin by exploring what I call prototype timing, which was fundamental in shaping my understanding of this message. Then I will explain how our bodies parallel the Old Testament temple to reveal how demons gain access to hidden areas. In chapters 4 and 5 I focus on common body parts that demons target and why. Then in chapter 7 I focus on several core rooms that we must recognize and target when praying for deliverance. In chapter 8 I will explain the four-step process for evicting these evil spirits, and in the final chapter I provide prayers for purging demons from common body parts that have not been addressed.

This book is for the individual seeking deliverance and the minister helping others get free. No matter what the issue, freedom is possible. My hope is that through the teaching in these pages, the eyes of your understanding will be opened to a whole new way of thinking about deliverance ministry. It is my desire that you will receive with an open heart the new paradigms and protocols God has shown me and, as a result, begin to expose these hidden demons so you and others can be completely set free.

God wants to take His church to a whole new level, and that journey begins here. But before we go any further, I want to pray for you.

> Heavenly Father, I ask that You would unlock the mysteries and secrets of deliverance to all who read this book. Open the eyes of their understanding and grant them insight into the revelation shared in these pages.
>
> Jesus Christ, I ask You to grant freedom to every person struggling with the deepest of bondage and most resistant demons. May You lay Your hands on those called to the ministry of deliverance and activate them with boldness to continue the work of setting the captives free!
>
> Holy Spirit, I ask You to impart a measure of faith to every reader who puts into practice what is written in this book. And I pray that You will

use this message to bring an upgrade to the ministry of deliverance for the body of Christ all over the world both now and in future generations! In Jesus's name, amen.

Chapter 1

THE MYSTERY OF PROTOTYPE TIMING

When the unclean spirit has gone out of a person, it passes through waterless places seeking rest, and finding none it says, "I will return to my house from which I came."
—Luke 11:24, esv

But when Jesus said "this temple," he meant his own body.
—John 2:21

H OW DO DEMONS take up residence in our body parts and the "rooms" of our souls? In order to answer that question, in this and the next chapter I want to explore some important parallels between the human body and the Old Testament temple. I don't intend to be dogmatic about the connections I'm about to show you, because the Lord often speaks to me in figurative language and I tend to communicate that way myself. But I do believe there are some significant spiritual insights for us to glean.

God first began to open my eyes to prototype timing through the writing of the apostle Paul. In his letter to the Corinthians, Paul wrote:

> For the law of Moses says, "You must not muzzle an ox to keep it from eating as it treads out the grain." *Was God thinking only about oxen when he said this? Wasn't*

> *he actually speaking to us? Yes, it was written for us, so that the one who plows and the one who threshes the grain might both expect a share of the harvest.*
>
> —1 CORINTHIANS 9:9–10, EMPHASIS ADDED

The verse Paul is quoting is Deuteronomy 25:4: "You must not muzzle an ox to keep it from eating as it treads out the grain." But Paul says, "Was God thinking only about oxen when he said this? Wasn't he actually speaking to us? Yes, it was written for us…"

Within Paul's statement we find the core of what I call "prototype timing." A *prototype* is "an original model on which something is patterned."[1] When God spoke about oxen in Deuteronomy 25:4, He wasn't thinking only of the animal. In his revelation Paul says, "It was written for us." This suggests that God had Paul's audience in mind when He communicated the laws concerning oxen to Moses. Thousands of years after the Book of Deuteronomy was written, Paul revealed that the oxen were actually a prototype for those laboring for God.

The oxen represented something that would be revealed at a later time—ministers of the gospel—and served as a model for how we are to understand the way ministers should be treated. So now whenever I see *oxen* in Scripture, I consider how the passage might relate to ministers of the gospel.

This is the essence of prototype timing. Throughout Scripture there are truths like this, objects and items that represent something that would be revealed at a later time. When God opened my eyes to these prototypes, I began to see a whole new layer of revelation in God's Word.

THREE KEY PROTOTYPES

Through prototype timing we can begin to see the revelation in this book unfold. By understanding three key prototypes, we will see how demonic spirits can reside in a person's body parts and especially how they can hide in "rooms" in our souls.

House

The word *house* can be found more than two thousand times in Scripture, and its first reference is in the Book of Genesis in the account of Noah and the building of the ark. As we will discuss in chapter 2, the ark parallels the temple in that it had many rooms and chambers. But to truly understand this prototype, we must first read Luke 11:24 (ESV):

> When the unclean spirit has gone out of a person, it passes through waterless places seeking rest, and finding none it says, "I will return to my house from which I came."

The demon said it would "return to my house from which I came." The demon was looking to go back to the "house" where it had been legally living, but earlier the verse said, "When the unclean spirit has gone out of a *person*" (emphasis added). The verse is telling us that the person is the house. This is why whenever I see *house* in Scripture, I consider how the verse may apply to a person.

Doing this has opened up a floodgate of hidden pearls—too many to include them all here. But I will share one that is found in Leviticus 14:33–34:

> Then the LORD said to Moses and Aaron, "When
> you arrive in Canaan, the land I am giving you as
> your own possession, I may contaminate some of the
> houses in your land with mildew."

In its proper exegesis the curse in Leviticus 14:34 is only mildew. But when I consider the passage more figuratively through the lens of prototype timing, where *house* represents a person, I realize the curse could be spiritual contamination. Though God does not "contaminate" a person with demons, this verse suggests that an individual can become spiritually polluted or unclean. We know this is true because 2 Corinthians 7:1 says, "Let us cleanse ourselves from everything that can defile our body or spirit. And let us work toward complete holiness because we fear God."

Seeing Leviticus 14:34 in light of prototype timing causes it to take on another layer of meaning. And I believe there are gems like this throughout the Bible. There is a vast deposit of hidden revelation in Scripture that is waiting to be discovered. The Bible says in Proverbs 25:2 that it's the glory of God to conceal a matter, but it's the glory of kings to search the matter out. Ask the Holy Spirit to give you the heart of a king to search out new revelation in Scripture!

Tabernacle

In the Book of Exodus, God instructed Moses to build Him a tabernacle according the pattern He showed him on Mount Sinai:

> Have the people of Israel build me a holy sanctu-
> ary so I can live among them. You must build this

Tabernacle and its furnishings exactly according to
the pattern I will show you.
                                        —EXODUS 25:8–9

In the next several verses God outlined exactly how He
wanted the tabernacle to be built and everything that should
be in it, from the type of material to be used to the exact
dimensions the furnishings should have. Why would God be
so particular? It's because the Hebrew word translated "tabernacle" means "residence" or "dwelling"[2]—again, a house!—
and this dwelling would belong to God.

In Exodus 25 the tabernacle referred to the place where
God Himself would dwell, but in the New Testament Peter
would use the same word to refer to his body: "Yea, I think
it meet, as long as I am in this tabernacle, to stir you up by
putting you in remembrance; knowing that shortly I must
put off this my tabernacle, even as our Lord Jesus Christ
hath shewed me" (2 Pet. 1:13–14, KJV). So *tabernacle* can also
refer to the human body.

The Old Testament tabernacle consisted of three compartments: the outer court, where the sacrifices, offerings,
and ceremonial cleansing of the priests were conducted;
the holy place, which housed the table of showbread, the
altar of incense, and the golden candlestick; and the most
holy place, where the ark of the covenant was kept. This is
also where once a year the high priest would enter with the
blood of atoning sacrifice to cleanse the children of Israel for
another year.

These three compartments also represent the three areas
of mankind: body (outer court), soul (inner court), and spirit
(most holy place). Incidentally the Lord desires for us to love

Him wholeheartedly in each of those areas. He says in Deuteronomy 6:4–5, "Listen, O Israel! The LORD is our God, the LORD alone. And you must love the LORD your God with all your heart [most holy place], all your soul [inner court], and all your strength [outer court]."

The tabernacle of Moses was God's mobile dwelling place on earth. The Israelites took it with them during their wilderness journey and when they crossed the Jordan River and entered the land of Canaan. But as Jeremiah 31:33 indicates, God never wanted to dwell in a tabernacle built by human hands. He desired to dwell in the human heart and cause us to be living tabernacles who carry the light of His presence to a dark world. (See 1 Corinthians 3:16.) But before this would happen through the death and resurrection of Jesus, the tabernacle of Moses would be replaced by something more sophisticated: the temple.

Temple

The Israelites worshipped God in the mobile tabernacle for years. Then when David was king of Israel, he began making plans to build a permanent habitation for God. Because David's hands had been stained with blood after years of war, the task of building a permanent temple would fall to his son Solomon (1 Chron. 28:6).

Before David died, he gave Solomon the blueprints he had drawn for building the temple:

> Then David gave Solomon the plans for the Temple and its surroundings, including the entry room, the storerooms, the upstairs rooms, the inner rooms, and the inner sanctuary—which was the place of

> atonement. David also gave Solomon all the plans he
> had in mind for the courtyards of the LORD's Temple,
> the outside rooms, the treasuries, and the rooms for
> the gifts dedicated to the LORD.
>
> —1 CHRONICLES 28:11–12

David spent much of his reign developing plans for the place where God's name would dwell forever. David had such an intimate relationship with the Lord that God called David "a man after my own heart" (Acts 13:22). I believe that because of his closeness to God, David figured out that God's ultimate desire was to dwell in the human heart. I believe he knew that one day the temple would not be the place where God's people went to make blood sacrifices; rather, it would be the place where His children worshipped God from a surrendered heart.

The Spirit of God would have had to reveal this to David, but Jesus made this truth plain in a conversation recorded in the Gospel of John:

> The hour is coming when neither on this mountain
> nor in Jerusalem [a reference to the temple because
> that is where it was located] will you worship the
> Father….God is spirit, and those who worship him
> must worship in spirit and truth.
>
> —JOHN 4:21, 24, ESV

After David died and Solomon became king, one of the first things Solomon did was ask God to give him wisdom. He knew that not only was the responsibility of leading the people of Israel on his shoulders but also the construction of the temple. His request so delighted the Lord that God granted him more wisdom than anyone who had ever lived. (See 2 Chronicles 1.)

I believe that supernatural wisdom was evident in the building of the temple. Solomon's temple was an upgrade of the previous tabernacle. The old tabernacle consisted only of three areas, but the new temple would include a three-story complex with ninety rooms. We will explore the blueprint of Solomon's temple in chapter 2, but here is where we see the emergence of rooms in the temple.

Thousands of years after Solomon built the temple, Jesus entered a rebuilt version of that facility and began turning over the tables of the merchants who were profiteering in God's house. When asked by the leading Jewish priests to show them a miraculous sign to validate His authority, Jesus replied, "Destroy this temple, and in three days I will raise it up" (John 2:19).

The leading priests responded by saying, "It has taken forty-six years to build this Temple, and you can rebuild it in three days?" (John 2:20). They didn't understand what Jesus was actually saying. We read in the next two verses:

> But when Jesus said "this temple," *he meant his own body.* After he was raised from the dead, his disciples remembered he had said this, and they believed both the Scriptures and what Jesus had said.
>
> —JOHN 2:21–22, EMPHASIS ADDED

When Jesus referred to the temple, He was talking about a body, not a building. This has opened a whole new realm of fresh revelation and unexplored scriptures to me, as every time I read the word *temple* in the Bible, I not only think of a physical building that was used as a place of worship, but I also consider how the passage might relate to the human body.

I love this passage about Jesus cleansing the temple in John 2 because it is a foreshadowing of deliverance. Just as Jesus walked in and cleared the money changers from the temple, He can step in and cleanse your temple. It doesn't matter how long you've been oppressed by bad habits, strongholds, or deeply rooted demonic activity, God can set you free in no time. He can undo in days what it took the devil years to create! It doesn't take the Lord that long to deliver; we're the ones slowing down the process when we refuse to surrender every area of our lives to Him.

It's worth repeating that it was never God's intent to dwell in temples made with human hands but in temples made without hands. (See Acts 17:24–26.) The terms of the new covenant are that if we choose to follow Christ, God will make His dwelling in our hearts:

> "But this is the new covenant I will make with the people of Israel after those days," says the LORD. "I will put my instructions deep within them, and I will write them on their hearts. I will be their God, and they will be my people."
> —JEREMIAH 31:33

This was God's design all along, even back when He outlined the blueprints of the tabernacle to Moses. The house, tabernacle, and temple were prototypes God would use to reveal His ultimate plan to make *us* His temple and establish a new covenant not just with the nation of Israel but with the whole world.

THE FULLNESS OF TIME

God was silent for four hundred years between the Book of Malachi and the Gospel of Matthew. Then He raised up a voice crying in the wilderness, proclaiming, "Prepare the way of the Lord." This voice was John the Baptist, the forerunner and herald for the One who would come after him—the promised Deliverer.

When Jesus appeared, the Bible says it was "the fullness of time" (Gal. 4:4, ESV). It was the perfect time for Jesus to come into the earth realm and speak about the kingdom of God. The Jewish people were living under the control of the Roman Empire and thus had a unique understanding of the concept of kingdom. Though they were not living in Rome, they were being governed by Rome. So when Jesus spoke of being governed by another kingdom, the idea was not foreign to His listeners.

Jesus often referenced the kingdom of God and the temple in His parables, but I believe He spoke with the prototypes in mind. When Jesus spoke of the kingdom, He meant the governing influence of a king over a territory, and when He spoke of the temple, He meant the human body.

Jesus merged the truth about the temple and the kingdom when He said:

> The Kingdom of God can't be detected by visible signs. You won't be able to say, "Here it is!" or "It's over there!" For the Kingdom of God is already among you.
> —LUKE 17:20–21

The kingdom of God—the governing influence of God—is among us because we are His temple. (See 1 Corinthians 6:19.)

The prototypes we've discussed don't just point us to this truth. I believe they also reveal how our human temples function and how the enemy would seek to contaminate them. If we consider that Solomon's temple, which was built with a complex of ninety rooms on three floors, represents our human temples, we can begin to see how demons would be able to hide and function within a person undetected for long periods of time, maybe even years.

But Jesus is still the great Deliverer, and He wants to open our eyes to what might be lurking in our temples. In the next chapter we will look at the blueprint of Solomon's temple to discover how it reveals where demons like to hide. But before we go further, I want to ask the Holy Spirit to give you an extra measure of discernment so you will be able to see the hidden blueprints of the human body and, as a result, the areas of the human temple that may need deliverance.

> Holy Spirit, I ask You to expand the capacity of the readers' discernment by removing anything that would hinder them from gaining deeper understanding of Your truth. In Jesus's name, amen.

CHAPTER 2

THE BLUEPRINT
OF THE TEMPLE

Then the man told me, "These rooms that overlook
the Temple from the north and south are holy. Here
the priests who offer sacrifices to the LORD will eat
the most holy offerings. And because these rooms are
holy, they will be used to store the sacred offerings—the
grain offerings, sin offerings, and guilt offerings."
—EZEKIEL 42:13

IN MARK 5 we find Jesus crossing the Sea of Galilee into the region called Decapolis, which was a group of ten towns. Upon landing on the shore in the city of Gadara, He was confronted by a demoniac who terrorized the town and was quarantined in the cemetery. When the demonized man approached Him, Jesus commanded the spirit within him to identify itself, and it responded, "My name is Legion, because there are many of us inside this man" (Mark 5:9). A legion was about two thousand foot soldiers, which means there were thousands of demons inside this man.

For many years I didn't pay much attention to Mark 5, but over time I began to ask some tough questions: Where does Legion go inside of a man? And how can two thousand demons perform their specific functions if they're all housed in one area? These questions began to bother me as I read

21

passages such as Luke 11, where Jesus described the kingdom of darkness as an organized, structured army. Having two thousand demons dwelling in one area of the soul wouldn't allow that army to carry out their assignments. It's no different than having two thousand foot soldiers all standing in the living room of a house trying to carry out their orders. Jesus Himself said, "Any kingdom divided by civil war is doomed. A family splintered by feuding will fall apart. You say I am empowered by Satan. But if Satan is divided and fighting against himself, how can his kingdom survive?" (Luke 11:17–18).

These questions and many others led me to continuously ask the Lord, "Where does Legion go when entering a person?" I began to spend hours looking to answer this question. Then one day I was watching a movie called *I, Robot*, which is about a police officer in 2035 who is looking for a robot that might have committed a crime. In one scene the detective is searching for a clue using a hologram of his deceased victim. After each question the detective asked, the hologram would say, "My responses are limited. You must ask the right questions."[1] The detective finally adjusted his questions and eventually was able to find the answers he was seeking.

After I watched that scene, the Holy Spirit whispered in my ear that I'd been asking the wrong questions and I needed to adjust my question to get the right answer. I immediately went from asking where Legion goes inside a person to whether the human body is built to be inhabited by that many demons. I sensed that the answer could not be found in studying the tabernacle of Moses, the mobile tent the people used as they wandered in the wilderness. This left only one other possibility; I needed to study the temple Solomon built.

First Kings 6 gives a detailed description of the blueprints of Solomon's temple and its compartments. There are four areas found in 1 Kings 6:1–9 that we are going to examine in-depth to see clearly that human beings have many rooms in their souls where demons can hide.

The temple of Solomon was a massive facility for worship, with hundreds of workers, singers, cooks, priests, and more. (See Nehemiah 7:39–73.) As I studied the temple, I began to realize that it was not a "tent" like the tabernacle, but a "facility." When I upgraded my thinking about the temple, I began to see where Legion goes when entering a human soul.

Let's read from 1 Kings 6:

> It was in midspring, in the month of Ziv, during the fourth year of Solomon's reign, that he began to construct the Temple of the LORD.... The Temple that King Solomon built for the LORD was 90 feet long, 30 feet wide, and 45 feet high. The entry room at the front of the Temple was 30 feet wide, running across the entire width of the Temple. It projected outward 15 feet from the front of the Temple. Solomon also made *narrow recessed windows* throughout the Temple.
>
> He built a *complex of rooms* against the outer walls of the Temple, all the way around the sides and rear of the building. The complex was *three stories high*, the bottom floor being 7½ feet wide, the second floor 9 feet wide, and the top floor 10½ feet wide.... There were *winding stairs* going up to the second floor, and another flight of stairs between the second and third

floors. After completing the Temple structure, Solomon put in a ceiling made of cedar beams and planks....

Then the LORD gave this message to Solomon: "Concerning this Temple you are building, if you keep all my decrees and regulations and obey all my commands, I will fulfill through you the promise I made to your father, David. I will live among the Israelites and will never abandon my people Israel."

—1 KINGS 6:1–6, 8–9, 11–13, EMPHASIS ADDED

CAN DEMONS LIVE IN THE TEMPLE?

Before I break down the four areas noted in the passage, I find it necessary to address two questions that often spark controversy among believers: Can the "temple" have a demon in it, and can God and Legion inhabit the same place? I don't want to spend too much time on those questions, but to put it simply, yes. I do believe you can be owned by God but still have areas in your life that have demonic habitation (not possession, but cohabitation).

While demons are prohibited from dwelling inside a believer by the courtroom of heaven, they can legally gain access if they are given permission to enter. For those who may be unfamiliar with this idea and are worried about straying from sound doctrine, let's briefly consider some passages from Scripture that show how this is possible.

Birds in the heart

In Matthew 13 Jesus tells the parable of the sower:

> A farmer went out to plant some seeds. As he scattered them across his field, some seeds fell on a footpath, and *the birds came* and ate them.... The seed that fell on the footpath represents those who hear the message about the Kingdom and don't understand it. Then the evil one comes and snatches away the seed that was planted in their hearts.
>
> —MATTHEW 13:3–4, 19, EMPHASIS ADDED

What makes this parable different from so many others is that Jesus gives the interpretation so as not to leave it open for misunderstanding. We find Jesus explicitly saying that the "birds" discussed in this parable are actually the devil and his angels. In this parable we find the birds (devil) taking the Word right out of the hearts of the hearers. In order to remove a seed of the kingdom out of someone's heart, you would have to be allowed inside the heart. If a person who has received the Word is a believer, and the devil (bird) gained access to remove the Word, that Christian had a demon.

Here's another verse to support this view. In the account of Ananias and Sapphira, the apostle Peter exclaimed to Ananias in Acts 5:3, "Why have you let Satan fill your heart?" Nowhere in the Book of Acts do we find Ananias and Sapphira being labeled false brethren, because if they had been unbelievers, they would not have faced such severe judgment for lying about how much they gave the church when they sold their possessions. We find God dealing harshly with them because they were believers who allowed Satan, like the birds in Matthew 13, to enter their temple and snatch the seed of giving and replace it with a seed of deception, which ultimately cost them their lives.

Birds in the trees

In Matthew 13 we find Jesus mentioning birds in another parable about the kingdom.

> Here is another illustration Jesus used: "The Kingdom of Heaven is like a mustard seed planted in a field. It is the smallest of all seeds, but it becomes the largest of garden plants; it grows into a tree, and birds come and make nests in its branches."
>
> —MATTHEW 13:31–32

This parable sealed the deal for me regarding whether a genuine Christian could have a demon in his life. In order to fully understand this parable, you have to view it through Jesus's interpretation of the parable of the sower, which He shared earlier in the same chapter. The gospel of the kingdom is the seed, and in this parable the seed landed on "good ground" and was able to produce a full-grown tree. The parable goes on to say that this tree was fruitful enough to grow bigger than any other tree in the forest and attracted birds that wanted to make their nests within its branches.

I believe the tree represents the kingdom of God spreading in the earth and the believer who allows the kingdom to manifest in his or her life. But while many believe the birds attracted to this tree are only those seeking refuge and sustenance in the message of the kingdom, I believe the birds can also represent the evil influences that seek to prevent the kingdom of God from spreading in and through us, just as they did in the parable of the sower.

The stronger you grow as a believer in the kingdom, the more birds (demons) will attempt to make their nests among your branches (the various areas of your life). This is why we must continually allow the Holy Spirit to convict us and purge us of any evil influences in our lives until the Lord calls us home.

So can a genuine believer have a demon operating in an unsurrendered area of his life? The answer is 100 percent yes. Now, in the remainder of the chapter, we will explore the four main parts of Solomon's temple to begin to understand how and where demons like to hide.

THE NARROW-RECESSED WINDOWS

Earlier in the chapter we read that unlike the tabernacle Moses built, King Solomon's temple included more than the outer court, holy place, and most holy place. We find that Solomon "also made narrow recessed windows throughout the Temple" (1 Kings 6:4). This created more potential entry points for demons that had to be guarded. Not much emphasis has been given to guarding the windows of the temple (due to more emphasis being on guarding the door), but Jesus did allude to these windows when He said:

> Your eye is like a lamp that provides light for your body. When your eye is healthy, your whole body is filled with light. But when it is unhealthy, your body is filled with darkness. Make sure that the light you think you have is not actually darkness.
>
> —LUKE 11:34–35

Windows play a crucial role in a house because they allow light to enter. Without light, we would be forced to function in the dark. And that's where most believers are when it comes to knowing what's really going on in their temples—in the dark!

The word translated "eye" in Luke 11:34 is sometimes used to mean "the eyes of the mind" or "the faculty of knowing"—in other words, it is referring to our understanding.[2] The passage in Luke 11 is letting us know that if the windows of our temples are dirty, broken, or foggy, then the temple will be full of darkness, and darkness equals ignorance.

In 2 Corinthians 2:11 the apostle Paul said that we are not to be ignorant of Satan's devices "lest Satan should get an advantage of us" (KJV). Without proper lighting in the temple, the devil will take advantage of us, and he may begin to operate in an area of our lives for years without any interference.

Each window also is a potential opening that can allow demonic spirits entry to steal, kill, and destroy. (See John 10:10.) Ask the Holy Spirit right now to begin the process of cleaning the windows of your understanding so you can clearly see if there are any demons hiding in your temple, renounce their work, and take back what is rightfully yours.

I'm reminded of the blind man in Mark 8 who needed Jesus to clean his windows (eyes) twice because at the first touch, his vision was still foggy:

> Jesus took the blind man by the hand and led him out of the village. Then, spitting on the man's eyes, he laid his hands on him and asked, "Can you see anything now?"

> The man looked around. "Yes," he said, "I see peo-
> ple, but I can't see them very clearly. They look like
> trees walking around."
>
> Then Jesus placed his hands on the man's eyes
> again, and his eyes were opened. His sight was com-
> pletely restored, and he could see everything clearly.
>
> —MARK 8:23–25

What a perfect depiction of someone who is determined
to experience total restoration and deliverance! This man
was willing to let the Lord touch him as many times as was
needed for him to be made whole. As you discover how the
enemy may have gained access to your life, I want to encourage you to do whatever it takes to get free. If you have to go
through several deliverance sessions or attend several confer-
ences to finally get free, do it. It will be worth it!

Make every effort to have your windows (understanding)
cleaned by the renewing of your mind. (See Romans 12:1–2.)
You renew your mind by reading and meditating on God's
Word each day. When you do this, you will begin to see the
transformation God is requiring of you. Deliverance is not
a power encounter but a truth encounter! The more truth
you understand, the freer you become and the more any
areas (rooms) in your life where demons are hiding become
exposed and resolved. You can't find the prince of darkness
while you're walking in darkness. You need the sun of righteousness to shine His light through your windows.

Throughout the New Testament the devil is described
as a thief. The difference between a thief and robber is that
a robber, whether armed or unarmed, doesn't conceal his
intentions and will forcefully and openly take your things.

But a thief is subtle. He waits for a moment of vulnerability to quietly steal your belongings without using force. By the time you're aware you've been robbed, the thief is long gone.

The same can happen within our own temples when we leave a window unattended or don't take seriously the need to repair a broken one. We are inviting demons to make their homes in these areas. Check your windows and make sure they are clean so you can watch for intruders!

THE THREE FLOORS

Let's look further at the floor plan of the temple of Solomon as found in 1 Kings 6. One of the first things you're going to notice is that the temple was upgraded to consist of more compartments than the tabernacle of Moses. While the design was the same at its core, there was one addition to Solomon's temple that stands out:

> He [Solomon] built a complex of rooms against the outer walls of the Temple, all the way around the sides and rear of the building. *The complex was three stories high....* The rooms were connected to the walls of the Temple by beams resting on ledges built out from the wall. So, the beams were not inserted into the walls themselves.
>
> —1 KINGS 6:5–6

Solomon's temple had a three-story complex of rooms built around it, and there were winding stairs leading up to each level. In a temple with a three-story complex of rooms there is enough space for demons to take their time in finding a less active area in which they can function with little to no interference. Those of us who are homeowners know we don't spend time in every part of the house every day. Long periods of time can pass before we go into certain parts of the house. Weeks, sometimes months, can pass without my going into the basement, and years can go by before I go into the attic.

With this understanding, we can see how, if a person were negligent, a demon could set up headquarters in a certain area of his "house" and even claim ownership there. This is why when I am ministering deliverance, demons will begin to resist by saying, "We've been here a long time," or "This person belongs to us." So the idea that a demon might be hiding in the last room on the third floor of someone's "house" is highly plausible, and any attempt to remove it will be met with resistance.

But thank God that Jesus is the great Deliverer, and for this purpose was the Son of God manifested—that He might "destroy the works of the devil" (1 John 3:8). Neither Satan nor his demons are any match for Him who took away the keys of hell, death, and the grave; the One who also has all authority in heaven, on earth, and under the earth; the One who in His earthly ministry entered the temple, turned over the tables, and purged it of the money changers. Call on Jesus right now and ask Him to enter your temple and go to every floor and start purging!

The parallel between the three floors of Solomon's temple and the three floors of Noah's ark brings up another interesting gem. God told Noah:

> Build a large boat from cypress wood and waterproof it with tar, inside and out. Then construct decks and stalls throughout its interior. Make the boat 450 feet

long, 75 feet wide, and 45 feet high. Leave an 18-inch
opening below the roof all the way around the boat.
Put the door on the side, and build three decks inside
the boat—*lower, middle, and upper.*
                    —GENESIS 6:14–16, EMPHASIS ADDED

As I mentioned previously, the ark had three floors—
upper, middle, and lower decks—with each floor having
rooms to house the animals. Here's a question I need to
ask: Was Noah's ark sanctified for God's purpose? Yes! Was
Noah's ark a vessel of preservation for the continuation of
humanity? Yes! Did the ark have unclean animals housed in
many of the compartments on various floors of the ark? The
answer is also yes! (See Genesis 7:2.) If something as holy as
Noah's ark had something unclean living in it and yet the
ark was still able to fulfill its purpose, we have further evi-
dence that Christians can have demons oppressing them.

THE WINDING STAIRS

The third area of the temple I want to address is the winding stairs. It would be pointless to build a three-story temple if there was no way to go back and forth between each
floor. Not much is written about the stairs, so we must ask
the Holy Spirit to show us the deeper meaning of the stairs.

Stairways are like bridges that allow people (and demons)
to go from one level to another. They also serve as a path-
way to exit when danger is lurking. Before the invention of
elevators, the most effective way to go up and down a building was to take the stairs. Without them, neither the larg-
est megalithic structures of antiquity nor the skyscrapers
of today would have been fully accessible. Even the great

Tower of Babel could not have been built without stairs. The Bible says:

> Then they said, "Come, let's build a great city for ourselves with a tower that reaches into the sky. This will make us famous and keep us from being scattered all over the world."
>
> —GENESIS 11:4

Nimrod, the chief architect of the Tower of Babel, and those working with him had to have included stairs because without them the structure could not have been much taller than a human being. I think it's interesting that most renderings of the Tower of Babel depict it as one large structure with winding stairs. I mention Nimrod in this revelation because he represents a type of Satan, and those who helped construct the tower represent a type of demon. The devil also needs a way to go back and forth between floors and rooms. Without stairs the devil would be stuck at whichever floor he entered on and would not be able to go up or down. These winding stairs grant him access.

What's also interesting is that winding stairs look a lot like DNA's double helix. Could it be that DNA within the human body forms bridges and connectors that allow demons to transfer down the bloodline from one generation to the next and from one floor to the next? Whatever the answer to that question, we know the temple of Solomon had winding stairs throughout it that led from one floor to another, giving the priest easy access to perform his duties. This leads me to the fourth and most vital area of the temple for our study.

The Complex of Rooms

The complex of rooms was built along the sides of the temple. These rooms were not there for show; they were built to support the daily functions of the priesthood. They served as storage for temple utensils, priestly wardrobes, animal sacrifices, and tithes, and were used as living quarters for many of the priests. So, without these rooms, the daily priestly functions required by the Law of Moses could not have been carried out.

In the remainder of this chapter we will look at the number of rooms built, the levels they were on, and their purpose. As you read this material, I pray that the eyes of your understanding will be opened so you begin to see the parallels between Solomon's temple and the human body. As you see the correlation between the many chambers, areas, and levels of both temples, you will begin to see that deliverance is not an easy process. It requires the time and patience to carefully go through each area of the human soul to remove contamination caused by human irresponsibility, generational curses, faulty theology, wrong thinking, cultural bias, and yes, demons. So please read the next several pages carefully as they lay important groundwork for the rest of the book.

As previously mentioned, the temple of Solomon had three main compartments: the outer court, the holy place, and the most holy place. But there also was a complex of rooms built along the side of the temple. We already established that these rooms give demons such as Legion ample space to function with little to no resistance. So as I began to think about these rooms, I had two main questions: How many rooms are in the temple and how many rooms are on each floor?

After searching the Scriptures for hours, I found myself bumping into dead ends. Finally I gave up looking. Then one morning during my daily devotional I was reading from the Book of Ezekiel and, like sun rays peeking over the horizon at dawn, there was the answer to both my questions hidden in one verse being highlighted by the Spirit of God:

> These side rooms were built in three levels, one above the other, with *thirty rooms* on each level. The supports for these side rooms rested on exterior ledges on the Temple wall; they did not extend into the wall.
>   —EZEKIEL 41:6, EMPHASIS ADDED

The best way to describe what happened to me when I read this verse is that I had an experience like Saul of Tarsus did in Acts 9 when Ananias laid hands on him and scales fell from his eyes. It was as if the scales fell from the eyes of my understanding, and I discovered a hidden treasure in a field just the like in the parable in Matthew 13. It was as if the dark areas of my understanding were now illuminated and I was being shown a secret that had been hidden in plain sight. Just as Solomon's temple had ninety rooms housed in the inner court,[3] the human body—the temple of the Holy Spirit—has ninety "rooms" in the realm of our soul that affect our thinking, personality, and behavior.

Let me explain using the following chart:

TEMPLE OF SOLOMON	TEMPLE OF THE HOLY SPIRIT
Three areas: • Outer court • Inner court • Most holy place (or holy of holies)	Three areas: • Body • Soul • Spirit
Narrow recessed windows: • Throughout the temple • Allows ventilation and light	Five senses that serve as entry and exit points: • Eyes • Ears • Nose • Mouth • Skin, hair, and nails
Three levels of rooms	Three areas of the soul: • Mind • Will • Emotions
Thirty rooms on each floor (totaling ninety), with each dedicated to a specific purpose and function, including storage	Ninety rooms on the level of our souls that reflect our personality traits and various roles and functions in our lives (for me, that would be husband, father, brother, uncle, apostle, etc.)

The Book of Ezekiel goes into great detail to describe the purposes and functions of many of these rooms. Chapters 41 through 44 are filled with many references to help us better understand the importance of these rooms. In essence these rooms help make up the personality and character of the temple, just as each compartment of the human soul helps distinguish us from one another. We all have ears, a nose, a mouth, eyes, and skin, but our personalities and character have been assigned to the rooms we have on the inside. And each room has a unique role.

For example, my name is Alexander. I'm husband to my wife, Ibelize. I am father to my sons, Apollos and Xavier. I'm the pastor and founder of He Is Risen Tabernacle in the Bronx. And I'm an uncle, neighbor, Christian—the list goes on and on. Each of these roles represents a room, and certain rooms are more important than others. That's why Ezekiel 41 shows that the various rooms had different measurements:

> Each level was *wider* than the one below it, corresponding to the narrowing of the Temple wall as it rose higher. A stairway led up from the bottom level through the middle level to the top level. I saw that the Temple was built on a terrace, which provided a foundation for the side rooms. This terrace was 10½ feet high. The outer wall of the Temple's side rooms was 8¾ feet thick.
>
> —Ezekiel 41:7–9, emphasis added

We also see the different priorities placed on various rooms in Ezekiel 42:

> Then the man told me, "These rooms that overlook
> the Temple from the north and south are holy. Here
> the priests who offer sacrifices to the LORD will eat
> the most holy offerings. And because *these rooms are
> holy*, they will be used to store the sacred offerings—
> the grain offerings, sin offerings, and guilt offerings.
> —EZEKIEL 42:13, EMPHASIS ADDED

We see this in our lives as well. For instance, my role as a father is more important than my role as an uncle. Both are important but not *equally* important. My office as an apostle to deliverance is more important than my role as a neighbor in my community. While one affects those who live around me, people I will occasionally see and interact with, the other affects those set free by the ministry the Lord had given me, which can impact whole generations.

Certain rooms are more important than others, and certain rooms are more important to the enemy. In the coming chapters we will look in detail at which rooms the devil and his cohorts most seek to contaminate and why.

I believe that once we understand that our bodies are the temple of the Holy Spirit and that we have ninety rooms in our mind, will, and emotions, we can have a bit more compassion on ourselves and others. It took years for our temples to become what they are today, and cleansing them through deliverance will not be instantaneous but rather a process of going room by room to remove that which is unauthorized and put things back in order.

The great news is that we're not left to perform this task alone. Jesus said, "I won't leave you as orphans. I will go away and send you another Comforter, who is the Spirit of truth, and He will guide you into all truth." (See John 14:18 and 16:13.) The Lord is also raising up a new generation of deliverance workers who have been tried by fire and carry the weight of the Nazarite vow, meaning they walk in pure holiness and understand the secrets of the kingdom to help bring deliverance in even the most difficult cases.

Before we go on to explore how demons gain access to the temple, take a few moments to invite the Holy Spirit to guide you as you continue to receive the revelation in this book:

> *Holy Spirit, thank You for granting me the privilege of understanding the truths written in these pages and for bringing light to that which is hidden in the dark rooms of my life. As I read these words, I give You permission to go into every room of my temple and turn on all the lights. Spirit of truth, may my deliverance process begin even now as I continue to read this book. Thank You in Jesus's name!*

CHAPTER 3

UNDERSTANDING THE REGULATIONS AND PROCEDURES

And the LORD said to me, "Son of man, take careful notice. Use your eyes and ears, and listen to everything I tell you about the regulations concerning the LORD's Temple. Take careful note of the procedures for using the Temple's entrances and exits."
—EZEKIEL 44:5

IN EZEKIEL 44 God commanded the prophet to pay careful attention to the regulations concerning the temple and the procedures for using the entrances and exits for all three floors and the ninety rooms. These procedures govern how to grant and restrict the access to the temple. So in a sense Ezekiel was being made a "temple inspector," which is a position of great authority.

The person with the most power over a building isn't necessarily the building owner but the building inspector because the inspector has the authority to approve or deny occupancy. This is the authority God gave Ezekiel. And to ensure that he would be a good temple inspector, God took Ezekiel through a crash course, showing him how to close areas of the temple (bind) or approve them for access (loose).

He then told Ezekiel to teach the same to others. This book is designed to carry on the work of the prophet Ezekiel by showing those who desire deliverance or are called to help others receive their deliverance how to inspect the temple. I pray that as you continue reading these pages, God will give you true understanding of what's happening in your temple or in the life of those to whom you are ministering. May all areas not in agreement with the building codes (the Bible) be declared in violation and removed!

WISDOM AND DISCERNMENT

As I mentioned previously, when Solomon became king, he prayed for wisdom to lead the people of Israel, and God answered his prayer by making him wiser than any person who had ever lived. Solomon needed wisdom because he was not a priest, and as problems arose that were connected to the temple, he would have to make decrees that were in line with the procedures of the temple. The same is true of us. We need an extra measure of wisdom to discern what is happening in the temple and respond appropriately. Every situation is not the same, so we need divine wisdom to troubleshoot all potential dangers and threats.

By God's grace I've conducted more than four hundred deliverance sessions. If there is one thing I've learned, it's that everybody is not the same, and *using the same cookie-cutter formula in deliverance is legalism*! After I realized that, I prayed and fasted for two things to be given to me, and I want to encourage you to pray for the same:

1. Discernment of spirits

2. Supernatural wisdom

The gift of discernment of spirits is the ability to see into the spirit realm and know the origin of a problem. Wisdom is the ability to know what strategy is needed to resolve the problem. People's problems are not always easy to pinpoint or handle, especially when the root issue is a demon that's been hiding in an area for so long it's hard to distinguish it from the person's flesh.

Because wisdom and discernment are so important, I encourage you to use this prayer to ask the Holy Spirit to give you an extra measure of these two gifts:

> *Holy Spirit, You are the great illuminator. I ask You to give me an extra measure of wisdom to understand the procedures for using the temple exits and entrances. I also ask You to grant me the gift of discernment of spirits to be able to see the root cause of all violations within the temple. As I walk in Your authority, grant me the boldness to begin the inspection process! In Jesus's name, amen.*

THE ENTRANCES AND EXITS

The command given to Ezekiel was for him to take careful notice of the procedures for using the entrances and exits of the temple. This would require a thorough evaluation to identify where they are located, how they function, and each one's level of importance. In his evaluation Ezekiel was looking for:

- Doorways that allow something in (entrances)
- Doorways that allow something out (exits)

Knowing these two categories helps narrow down the root causes for demonic activity to two types: those things allowed to enter and those things not forced to leave. These two classifications are backed up by Matthew 18:18, when Jesus said, "Truly, I say to you, whatever you bind [don't allow] on earth shall be bound in heaven, and whatever you loose [allow] on earth shall be loosed in heaven" (ESV). Recognizing these categories will eliminate half of the excuses those seeking freedom often give and shorten the deliverance session from hours to less than an hour.

Oh, how I wish deliverance ministers would catch this revelation and shorten the sessions from five hours to thirty minutes. I'm amazed at how sensational, extreme, and heretical deliverance has become. It's no wonder many sober-minded pastors stay away from it. If I were on the outside looking in at much of what passes for deliverance ministry these days, I would stay away from it too! It can appear very unbiblical. I've seen some sessions that consisted of hours of endless yelling, vomiting, and other demonic manifestations that left the person, the deliverance minister, and the intercessors exhausted. The purpose of deliverance is to remove the burdens of those who are heavy laden, not add to them!

No More Guessing, Fishing, and Hoping

I want to pause here and say a word to deliverance ministers. God commanded Ezekiel to take notes, which implies that he was to study and learn. It also implies that he was to remember what he studied and learned. There will be times during a deliverance session or in your own self-deliverance when you will forget certain points and deliverance strategies.

Reviewing your notes is an effective tactic for when you get stuck. Taking notes also allows you to make changes when you learn something new. Nothing is more pointless than an ineffective method for deliverance.

The human body is always changing, and the tactics of the enemy are always evolving. What worked for a couple sessions might not work for the next. Jesus said in Mark 9:29 that some types of demons "cannot be driven out by anything but prayer" (ESV). This lets us know that some situations require different strategies.

If and when you encounter something you need to change, by keeping notes you will be able to remember what you learned and teach it to others. In our ministry after every deliverance session we sit down and discuss what happened. It's not to gossip but to sharpen our swords so we will be even better equipped for the next session.

Deliverance is not about fighting the darkness but turning on the light. It's finding the root cause of a problem with the lights on, not swinging aimlessly in the dark until you eventually hit a target. It's your job to administer deliverance from a place of knowing, not from a place of guessing, fishing, and hoping! These are the archenemies of true deliverance, and they are to be avoided at all costs.

Guessing

People who are completely ignorant of the ministry of deliverance but have been thrown into this area of ministry by the Holy Ghost or their peers may resort to mimicking what they have seen through the years. They may watch YouTube videos of deliverance sessions or they may watch the movie *The Exorcist* to get ideas (just kidding!). This method dishonors God the most and causes the kingdom of darkness to ridicule the minister during a session. If you find yourself unsure of what to do while in a deliverance session, don't guess. Quickly call in a more experienced person and ask that individual to continue the session as you remain to serve as an intercessor. Or gather a group of believers and form a chain around the person and pray for God to intervene. Trust me, God will not allow you to be embarrassed. The Bible says, "If the axe is dull and he does not sharpen its edge, then he must exert more strength. Wisdom has the advantage of giving success" (Eccles. 10:10, NASB).

Fishing

People who have some understanding of deliverance but minimal experience may not know how to accurately identify which demon is operating. Like a fisherman with bait, they resort to calling out a bunch of demons in hopes of eventually catching one. Most believers fall into this category because so many local churches don't embrace the ministry of deliverance—some churches don't even believe demons exist—and thus don't train believers in this area. When confronted with a tough, resistant demon, these individuals readily accept the challenge but soon realize that removing the demon will take more than five minutes. True deliverance requires skill and accuracy but is not limited by it, meaning there will be times when God will honor your fishing and remove a demon. After all, God honored the disciples' decision to cast lots to find someone to take Judas's place. (See Acts 1:26.) But He will eventually require you to mature!

Hoping

Some people are skilled and experienced in deliverance, but they don't know what to do in the face of prolonged resistance during a deliverance session. Instead of waiting on the Holy Spirit to reveal a strategy or even ending the session and resuming at a later date, they do whatever comes to mind and hope God honors their efforts by bringing breakthrough. Hoping is the most dangerous of all three enemies to deliverance because at its root is self-centeredness. The person who chooses to hope is more concerned about not looking foolish and powerless than in actually helping the person receive freedom! I pray that from this moment forward you will remember what I'm about say and let it be the driving force of every session you might be called upon to conduct: *deliverance is not about you*! Deliverance has always been about the ongoing work of Jesus to expand the kingdom of God on the earth. It's the military force of heaven to dismantle the works of darkness and the fallen angels who persuade it!

Don't let pride prevent someone from getting delivered. Don't just hope you land on the right strategy. Seek the Holy Spirit or stop the session and reschedule after you've had a chance to seek the Lord.

To avoid guessing, fishing, and hoping, we must do as God instructed Ezekiel and learn the regulations and procedures of the temple.

THE REGULATIONS AND PROCEDURES

God wants you to understand how your temple operates and what it needs to function properly. Just as you need to understand how a door lock works to get inside a house, you must understand what it will take to open and close doors to demons in the temple. Every door has locks, and those locks are opened with keys, not with yelling. Your authority doesn't increase with decibels; it increases with revelation (keys).

The sooner you understand the regulation of a door (how it works) and the procedure (strategy) to get it open, the sooner you can come out from the cold into a warm house. The same is true in deliverance. We must understand how to identify what's malfunctioning in a person's life, or in our own, and what's needed to heal it.

The prophet Ezekiel was instructed to listen to everything the Lord told him about the regulations concerning the temple and the procedures for the entrances and exits. These regulations and procedures are similar but different.

Regulations

The Hebrew word translated "regulations" in Ezekiel 44:5 is *chuqqah*, which means "that which is established or defined."[1] It comes from a root word that means "statute, ordinance…prescribed limit, boundary."[2] According to Merriam-Webster's dictionary, a *regulation* is also "a rule or order issued by an executive authority or regulatory agency of a government and having the force of law."[3] This concept is expressed in the Greek word *kanōn*, which means "rule or standard."[4] It's where the church gets the term *canon*. The canon is the authoritative list of books accepted as Holy Scripture—the books that present the rule or standard for everything we do as humans.

To know the regulations of the temple means we must

know what the devil can and cannot do in the human temple. We know that through the Word of God. As we discussed in chapter 2, even believers can allow demonic spirits inside their temple, but the key word is *allow*. I've said this before, but demons can enter a believer's life only when they are given legal access.

When we don't align our thoughts and confession with what God says in His Word and instead choose to agree with the enemy, we open a door to the enemy. When we choose to wallow in bitterness instead of walking in forgiveness, we open a door to the enemy. When we don't address generational curses, we open a door to the enemy. I've heard many people say, "The devil made me do it." They don't realize their actions and the fruit of those actions are a direct result of what they do or don't allow in their temple!

Just as we can give demons access to our temples, we must realize that we have been given authority through Christ to command them to leave. When we serve demons an eviction notice, they have to go. If they resist, you must ask the Holy Spirit to reveal whether something is allowing them to stay. If nothing is giving them legal access, they are trespassing and they will have to bow to your commands.

I saw a powerful demonstration of this when I was asked to lead a young lady who was bisexual through deliverance. This young lady was a believer in Christ and was genuinely seeking freedom. I agreed to see her, and on the date of her appointment she came to our office. About fifteen to twenty minutes into the session she began to fade in and out of consciousness, as if in a trance. Her eyes would roll back and her face would contort, which is a sign of a demonic presence.

The demon would stare at me like an enraged animal. Then the young lady would regain consciousness and be unaware of what was happening. This went on for another fifteen minutes, and I honestly didn't know what to do. Finally, after a couple of feeble attempts to regain control of the session, a holy boldness came upon me, and I stood on my feet, lifted my right hand to heaven, and declared, "Heavenly Father, may there be a sword placed in my hands to smite Your enemies."

The demon began to shriek and threw the woman on the ground. It began convulsing and screaming, "No!" I then proceeded to motion as if I was stabbing the demon, and to my surprise the demon began yelling for me to stop stabbing it. Those serving as intercessors during the session were as shocked as I was to see that God would give His children such authority. The young lady was delivered from the demon of lesbianism that day! Today she is married and has a beautiful child.

It's important to know your authority as a believer because if you don't enforce it, the demons will not voluntarily leave. They'll do whatever they can to remain where they are and continue to wreak havoc in a person's life. But whether or not they stay or go isn't up to them. Know your authority and walk in it confidently!

Once a demon has been removed, that space must be filled. We will address this at length in chapter 8, but for now I'll just say that we must release blessing or the opposite of whatever the demon's assignment was. Jesus said, "When an evil spirit leaves a person, it goes into the desert, seeking rest but finding none. Then it says, 'I will return to the person I came from.' So it returns and finds its former home empty, swept, and in order. Then the spirit finds seven other spirits more evil than itself, and they all enter the person and live there. And so that person is worse off than before" (Matt. 12:43–45). Empty spaces always fill up. Even in the natural, if you leave a room empty, eventually it will fill up with boxes and other items for storage. Once you evict a demon, decree that the empty space be filled with more of what is blessed, good, and holy!

There are regulations established in God's Word, and there are regulations that are part of human nature. While everyone is different and unique strategies are needed to help each person get free, all humans have the same fundamental needs within them. We all get hungry and thirsty, so we all need food and water. We all desire to be loved and validated, so we need to be affirmed and to connect with others. God has designed us all with fundamental needs that we need fulfilled in our lives. Knowing this can help us identify breaches. If a core need is not being met, the enemy can attempt to exploit that area of vulnerability. For instance, when people are not receiving love, they may open themselves up to dangerous and demonic activities to meet that need.

Again, no two people are alike, and no two deliverance sessions will be exactly the same. But understanding the regulations of the temple enables a person to work accurately and effectively when conducting self-deliverance or ministering deliverance to others, because there is no guessing, hoping, or fishing. It can also help you know when something is not a demon but rather an act of irresponsibility. Irresponsibility cannot be cast out; people must take responsibility for their actions through repentance and disciplining themselves to pray, fast, and study the Word.

Procedures

A *procedure* is "a particular way of accomplishing something" or "a series of steps followed in a regular definite order."[5] The word refers to a pattern or a particular system of functioning. For instance, the procedure of the human eye is to essentially take a picture of what you see and send that image to your brain, which discerns what the object is. If there is a malfunction during any part of the process, you will not be able to see properly.

The same is true in the human temple. Any malfunction can permit the entry of a demon, which will creep in like the thief described in John 10. Jesus said the thief will enter the sheepfold through some way other than the gate (v. 1). This is exactly what demons will do if any area of the temple is not functioning correctly or if the entrances and exits are left unattended.

For example, a broken spirit can leave a wide-open window for a demon of depression and hopelessness to fly in and rob a person of peace. A moment of rage can open a door to allow bitterness and unforgiveness to enter. This is why the devil is always seeking to push our buttons, because he knows how we react to situations and he will exploit any opportunity he is given. The primary strategy of familiar spirits—spirits that are familiar with a person and a family and manifest from generation to generation—is to push the same buttons to get the same responses. They are masters of procedures and will work tirelessly to consistently push those buttons to get the same pattern of movement every time.

When doing deliverance, we must seek supernatural wisdom and discernment regarding the procedure needed to address whatever is malfunctioning. Ignorance is the archenemy of deliverance. I have conducted hundreds of deliverance sessions with a very high success rate. It's not because I'm special but because I'm consistently updating my understanding of the procedures needed during each deliverance session. My strategy for deliverance adjusts when God grants me more insight. Until then I keep executing the last procedure, and I get the same results.

One time during a deliverance session someone struggling with his sexual orientation was having a hard time breaking through, and my deliverance workers were making slow progress. I decided to join the session, and immediately the demon wanted to attack me. I clearly heard the Holy Spirit tell me to stand there quietly and not say anything but to love on this person. Although the person was obviously demonized, the procedure in that moment was not confrontation but a demonstration of love. This person was locked inside a room in his soul (a topic we will address at length in chapter 6), and the only way it could be accessed was through gentleness. The reason the workers were not gaining ground was because they were violating the protocols that governed that area of his life.

After about ten minutes of just calmly loving this person with no confrontation, he burst out in tears and hugged me. Then the demon left. There is no cookie-cutter, one-size-fits-all formula for addressing the various areas of the temple.

But if you allow the Holy Spirit to show you the procedures when people stand before you, you will find deliverance happens so much more easily and quickly.

Those seeking freedom through our ministry don't always get delivered of everything they're dealing with during one session, but they always get free from something. When I find we can't move past something during a deliverance session that is intended to address a specific demon or curse, I know I need more insight into that area. I won't continue until I find the new strategy needed to help the person get free. (In the next chapter we will look at specific entrances and exits and how to cleanse each one.)

Even as you read this, you may be saying that you're a hard case and it's easier for others to get set free than it is for you. The devil is a liar! While other deliverance ministers may have given up on you, your case is not impossible. You can learn how to open even the most obstinate rooms, doors, and windows in your life.

The Holy Spirit is amazing. I am typing with tears in my eyes because there was a time when I thought I was a hopeless case. Then I got delivered, and here I am writing a book that will help others like me get set free! I decree that every door will break open, every window will crack open, every area in your life that says "Do Not Enter" will break open, and the Holy Spirit will sweep the house and set you free.

Fortunately understanding how demons access our lives and where they hide does not have be a mystery. God made it clear in the blueprint He outlined in Scripture.

CHAPTER 4

IDENTIFYING DEMONIC ENTRANCES AND EXITS

Son of man, describe to the people of Israel the Temple I have shown you....Let them study its plan....Describe to them all the specifications of the Temple—including its entrances and exits—and everything else about it. Tell them about its decrees and laws. Write down all these specifications and decrees as they watch so they will be sure to remember and follow them.
—EZEKIEL 43:10–11

IN THE BOOK of Ezekiel, God not only commands the prophet to learn the procedures of the entrances and exits of the temple, but also to study the plan, or blueprint. This command reminds me of the owner's manual that comes with a new electronic product. The manual explains the purpose and function of every button, but most people (especially men) don't take time to read the instructions. Instead, we try to figure out how to operate the device on our own. An hour later, after many futile attempts to understand how the machine works, we turn to the manual for answers. (You may be laughing right now because you've been there!)

The Bible is humanity's "owner's manual," and within its pages are explanations for every part of human life, including the entrances and exits demons use to wreak havoc in our lives.

BE SPECIFIC

Certain methods in the ministry of deliverance from the 1970s are outdated. Since that time the body of Christ has been taught only how to generally identify demons and remove them. This has left the church at a disadvantage because we haven't mastered the specifics. Effective deliverance requires us to identify the specific issue and address it with precision. Generic warfare prayers will work when you're first starting out in deliverance, but there will come a time when God will require you to be more targeted in your prayers and decrees.

If you don't mature out of generalities, you'll eventually repeat the story of Mark 9 when the disciples tried every method but couldn't cast the demon out of the young epileptic boy. When the disciples asked Jesus why they couldn't cast the demon out, He said in essence, "This particular kind requires a particular strategy." (See Mark 9:29.) Looking more closely at this case, we find Jesus asking the young boy's father about the history of the child. Why? Jesus was troubleshooting to target His prayers. In this chapter I am going to explain with specificity the entrances and exits of our temples and how the devils enter.

This chapter is one of the most important in this book. We are following the command given to the prophet Ezekiel to study the plan of the temple and describe the specific functions of the entrances and exits and how the enemy gains access to these areas (sometimes even controlling them). There is a blessing in knowing that our obedience will be rewarded by the manufacturer of the human soul—the God of Abraham, Isaac, and Jacob.

This chapter will provide a breakdown of the basic entrances and exits, which are the most vulnerable areas. Then chapter 5 will offer a close look into several other key parts of the human anatomy that frequently become fortified strongholds that require targeted deliverance. In chapter 9 I will include prayers that address various body parts not included in either of these chapters. I do this because I want you to be fully prepared to root out every hidden demon and serve it an eviction notice.

Any prayer I include for removing a demon is intended to be said out loud. At the least it should be written, or if you're leading someone through deliverance you can have the person nod his head to acknowledge agreement. However it is done, the demon must be repudiated openly (something I will address fully in chapter 8) because demons don't read minds and exposing them openly will deactivate their authority.

The reason God wanted His church to study the plan of the temple was so we would know how each part was intended to be used and how it can be misused. There are more body parts to explore and more revelation to receive concerning them than I have included in this book, but I believe this will be a helpful beginning. This chapter is lengthy but informative. So let's get started.

THE MOUTH AND LIPS

The mouth is both an entrance and an exit, and it is one of the most important parts of our bodies. According to some sources, when the Bible says in 1 Corinthians 15:45 that Adam became a "living soul," it means he became a "speaking spirit."[1] What distinguishes mankind from the rest of God's creation is our ability to speak intelligently. This privileged ability to communicate verbally allows us to expand and establish God's kingdom on the earth.

We have been given authority enforced by the court-room of heaven, where angels, demons, and even God listen intently to our words. Jesus told the disciples that they had been given keys to the kingdom, and whatever they bound on earth (locked up with their words) would be enforced in heaven, and whatever they loosed on earth (unlocked through their words) also would be enforced in heaven. (See Matthew 18:18.) When a person renounces (out loud) demonic activity, declaring that it must cease and be removed from his life, a spiritual "motion" is processed and swiftly enforced in heaven. All demons have to obey it and be expelled!

This is one reason that of all the body parts, the mouth is the area demons target the most. Through the more than four hundred deliverance sessions I have been involved in, I have found that deliverance can be narrowed down to one thing: the exchange of words. Many times during deliverance, I've seen demons work hard to keep people from declaring any words that would cancel the demonic influence or allow the Holy Spirit to enter that space. You may have heard this before, but it is indeed true: your biggest fight is with your mouth.

The Bible says that "death and life are in the power of tongue" (Prov. 18:21, MEV). Through our words, we give demons legal access to our lives! If our confession is negative, full of worry, evil, unwholesome, etc., we will open wide the doors to demonic spirits that can only gain access if we give them permission. Words give demons power! But the great news is that same way our words open the door, our words can also close the door and deny demons entry if we speak those things that are true, just, and lovely, as Philippians 4:8 instructs. When you change your confession, you'll see the devil flee!

Because the kingdom of darkness is aware of the power of words, demons like to set up camp in the mouth area, especially on the lips and tongue. (I will address the tongue separately in the next chapter because it is such a key target of the enemy.) The Bible says, "The poison of asps is under their lips" (Rom. 3:13, KJV). Demons hide in the mouth and lip area and are consistently at work to make sure the believer is speaking words that bring destruction, negativity, and despair. Other manifestations of demons in the mouth and lip area include blasphemy, gossip, seduction, homosexuality (oral sex), lying, cursing, negative talk, smoking, and any other sins that specifically use the lips and mouth.

Decree freedom in this part of the body by saying this prayer out loud:

> Heavenly Father, You created my mouth to worship, bless, encourage, uplift, communicate, sing, and tell of Your goodness. Please forgive me for using my mouth in ways that don't glorify You. [Insert any other inappropriate uses of the tongue that the Holy Spirit reveals.] I repent and I dedicate my mouth to You.
>
> Holy Spirit, please reveal to me the sins I've committed and the doors I've opened with my mouth so

I can close them now. I command every demon that
has attached itself to my mouth and lips to detach
itself now in Jesus's name. I order you to leave now
in the name of Jesus.

Lord Jesus, touch my mouth now and heal it. I
decree that from this moment forward I will speak
blessing, healing, forgiveness, and expansion, and
my words will be like honey to those who hear them.
In Jesus's name, amen. [Or you can continue praying as the Holy Spirit guides you.]

THE EYES

The eyes are an entrance the enemy attempts to use to shape
our thinking. Luke 11:34 says, "Your eye is the lamp of your
body. When your eye is healthy, your whole body is full of
light, but when it is bad, your body is full of darkness" (ESV).
The eyes are called the lamp of the body because they have
the ability to bring light, truth, love, insight, illumination,
and revelation.

The biggest issue when it comes to the eyes is lust. The
Bible says, "For all that is in the world, the lust of the flesh,
and *the lust of the eyes*, and the pride of life, is not of the Father,
but is of the world" (1 John 2:16, KJV, emphasis added).

Lust is never satisfied. It has *no* restraint or boundar-
ies. Lust can't be tamed or controlled; it has to be crucified
when it rears its ugly head. Proverbs 27:20 says that "the eyes
of man are never satisfied" (KJV). This is why we must diligently guard what we watch and fix our attention on, because
the potential to lust will be present as long as we can see.

You may think it's a bit of a stretch to say that a demon

can dwell in someone's eyes, but let's look again at 1 John 2:16. It says "the lust *of* the eyes," not the lust of the person. "Of the eyes" means the eyes have their own lust. People sin, but a demonic spirit residing in a body part can magnify a person's desire for something. This is why it can become so difficult to stop ungodly behavior even when the desire to do so is strong.

When a man says he has a wandering eye, believe him! That doesn't give him an excuse to sin. But if there is a demon lodging in his eyes, then he may need targeted deliverance prayer to remove the demon. Also keep in mind that you could be dealing with a person who has spent many years looking at things in a certain way, storing multiple layers of lust in his or her memory.

Many times during deliverance sessions I've seen demons hiding in the person's eyes. It's the body part that most frequently reveals the presence of demonic activity. The eyes usually glaze over and the person will have a blank stare. Sometimes the eyes get bloodshot or turn black, or the eyes will contort, revealing that you're no longer looking at the person seeking freedom but at a demon. The demon oftentimes won't look at you, and sometimes it will cause the person's eyes to take on an animallike quality.

Besides lust, other manifestations of demonic activity in the eyes are seduction, a wandering eye, vanity, judgment, jealousy, false perceptions, pornography consumption, excessive social media use, and excessive television viewing. But there is a wide-open door for the eyes to lust after anything. Decree freedom in this body part by saying this prayer out loud:

> *Father of creation, my eyes belong to You. My sight*
> *belongs to You. My vision belongs to You. My eyes*
> *bring light to my body. I clean the windows of*
> *my eyes now in the name of Jesus. I come against*
> *every manifestation of demonic activity in my eyes,*
> *including illness. I decree perfect vision and freedom*
> *from cataracts, eye problems, and any eye disease*
> *that may attempt to manifest now or in the years*
> *to come. I decree that I have the eyesight of eagle*
> *in Jesus's name. I know my eyes are the door to the*
> *heart, so I ask You to help me guard my eyes with*
> *all diligence* (Prov. 4:23). *I repent of and renounce*
> *all forms of lust I have allowed in my life, and I cast*
> *down every lustful thought in the name of Jesus. I*
> *declare that I will think upon those things which are*
> *pure, honest, and of a good report* (Phil. 4:8) *in the*
> *name of Jesus. Amen.* [Or you can continue pray-
> ing as the Holy Spirit guides you.]

THE EARS

The ears have the singular purpose of allowing a person to hear, making them an entrance to the body. Many times in Scripture God tells the children of Israel that if they hear His voice, not to harden their hearts. (See, for example, Psalm 95:1–70.) There are specific demons that target this body part, namely the deaf and dumb spirit. (See Mark 9:25.) These demons seek to make a person dull of hearing and unable to discern God's voice, because their ultimate goal is to lead the individual to develop a reprobate mind.

Hearing is extremely important; for a believer in Christ

it's more important than seeing. God repeatedly calls us to hear His voice, His commands, and His words. Hearing should be a natural function of the believer, as Jesus said, "My sheep hear my voice, and I know them, and they follow me" (John 10:27, ESV). The Bible goes a step further and says that "if the trumpet give an uncertain sound, who shall prepare himself to the battle?" (1 Cor. 14:8, KJV). Without the ability to hear properly, we can't be prepared for war.

The parable of the sower in Matthew 13 describes four types of hearers of the message of the kingdom.

> The seed that fell on the footpath represents those who hear the message about the Kingdom and don't understand it. Then the evil one comes and snatches away the seed that was planted in their hearts. The seed on the rocky soil represents those who hear the message and immediately receive it with joy. But since they don't have deep roots, they don't last long. They fall away as soon as they have problems or are persecuted for believing God's word. The seed that fell among the thorns represents those who hear God's word, but all too quickly the message is crowded out by the worries of this life and the lure of wealth, so no fruit is produced. The seed that fell on good soil represents those who truly hear and understand God's word and produce a harvest of thirty, sixty, or even a hundred times as much as had been planted!
>
> —MATTHEW 13:19–23

This is why demons will attack your ability to hear in the Spirit. You can't follow the Good Shepherd if you can't hear Him. The enemy has demons assigned to keep your inner ear distracted. They block sound from entering by closing the ears to any outside influence. They want you to hear only Satan's lies. But Jesus wants to bring deliverance to your ears and remove the demons blocking your hearing.

Luke 11:20 says, "But if it is by the finger of God that I cast out demons, then the kingdom of God has come upon you" (ESV). In the text the finger of God represents the manifestation of the kingdom through deliverance. In the New Testament we find Jesus healing a deaf man by putting His fingers in his ears:

> After he took him aside, away from the crowd, Jesus put his fingers into the man's ears. Then he spit and touched the man's tongue. He looked up to heaven and with a deep sigh said to him, "Ephphatha!" (which means "Be opened!").
>
> —MARK 7:33–34, NIV

If the finger of God represented deliverance and Jesus put His fingers in the ears of a deaf man, then Jesus was ministering deliverance to this man's ears! As Jesus said in Matthew 11:15, "He that hath ears to hear, let him hear" (KJV).

Decree freedom in this body part by saying this prayer out loud.

> *Holy Spirit, my ears were meant to be instruments to hear Your voice. I ask that You reveal to me the things that are blocking me from hearing You.* [Write down what the Holy Spirit reveals, then proceed to verbally renounce those things.]
>
> *Father, I repent of* _____ [go through the list of things the Holy Spirit revealed]. *I renounce*

any involvement in this activity and sever any curse attached to it now in Jesus's name. I declare my ears open to hear Your voice, open to receive new revelation, open to hear Your plans and purposes. I release the voice of the Lord over my ears now in Jesus's name! Amen. [Or you can continue praying as the Holy Spirit guides you.]

THE NOSE

The nose has a dual purpose as both an entrance and exit. The nose is by far the most amazing of all the body parts, yet it is the most overlooked during deliverance. The Bible has a lot to say about the nose and the nostrils. Certain aromas were pleasing to God (Gen. 8:21; Num. 15:3; Ezek. 20:41) while others were a stench to Him (Isa. 65:5), and when He was angry, "Smoke poured from his nostrils" (2 Sam. 22:9).

The nose in Scripture represents discernment. I once saw a documentary about the nose that said there is a level of taste that's directly connected to smelling.[2] The nose also is used as a channel for breathing. The nose is to the mouth as Eve was to Adam. It is a helpmeet that assists us with breathing while we eat. It's also a passageway for spiritual activity.

We find that God breathed the "breath of life" into Adam's nostrils:

> Then the LORD God formed the man from the dust of the ground. He breathed the breath of life into the man's nostrils, and the man became a living person.
>
> —GENESIS 2:7

This text is the primary basis for seeing the nose as a gateway for spirits to travel back and forth in the human temple. Demonic spirits will use the nose as a backdoor to enter the body. That is why the nose ring signifies ownership. (See Ezekiel 16:6–14.)

In addition to nose rings, which signify bondage to the occult, witchcraft, antichrist, rebellion, anarchy, etc., signs and symptoms of demons hiding in the nose include:

- Persistent sinus problems that doctors can neither identify nor control

- Drug addiction (particularly to drugs that are inhaled)

- Uncontrollable sneezing when under stress

- Feelings of insecurity about one's nose (If a person has a large nose, the demon of insecurity can dwell on the nose, making the person feel insecure about how others perceive his nose.)

Decree freedom in this body part by saying this prayer out loud:

> *Father, You breathed life into man, and our nostrils are the gateways for Your life-giving Spirit. I ask You to reveal anything attached to my nose that may be hindering this life from flowing—any sickness, disease, or irritation coming from a demonic source. I come against* _____ [insert whatever the Holy Spirit reveals] *hidden within my nose and sinuses. I order every demon hiding to leave my*

*nose area now in the name of Jesus. Father, let Your
healing virtue flow upon my nose and bring total
restoration. In Jesus's name, amen.* [Or you can
continue praying as the Holy Spirit guides you.]

Deliverance through breathing gateways

It is important to understand that demons can enter and
exit a body through breathing gateways (mouth, nose, throat,
lungs, and even the breath itself). The Greek word translated "spirit" in the Bible is synonymous with "breath."[3] God
breathed into Adam's nostrils, and he became a "living soul"
(Gen. 2:7, KJV). Demonic spirits also travel in and out of the
body through the breath, completely undetected by those
who don't realize that the battle is fought at this level and
that inhaling and exhaling can be strategies of war.

The symbolism of inhaling and exhaling can be found all
over Scripture, from Adam becoming a living soul to God
scattering His enemies with the breath of His nostrils. I
explain inhaling and exhaling this way:

- Inhale—the act of receiving
- Exhale—the act of removing

In my experience when a demon enters the body through
inhaling, the person will cough uncontrollably. And when a
demon leaves the body through exhaling, the person usually
vomits or sneezes. When conducting a deliverance session, I
coach people to breathe in and out, and then I audibly tell the
demon, "You're unclean, demon! Every time [person's name]
breathes, you ride that breath and come out of this body in
Jesus's name." This technique might seem farfetched, but it

works. If done with faith, there will always be breakthrough because demons know the rules, and they obey them.

We see an example of a spirit being released through exhaling in the crucifixion of Christ at Calvary. When He had accomplished all that needed to be done on the Cross, the Bible says, "Jesus shouted out again, and he released his spirit" (Matt. 27:50). What we see is Jesus releasing His spirit with an exhale. Of course, Jesus was not releasing a demon, but demons can travel out of a person in the same way. Exhaling is a powerful tool that can be used during the deliverance process.

The mystery of a sneeze

In the Bible we find only one verse that uses the word *sneeze*, and it is when the prophet Elisha raised the Shulamite woman's son from the dead. When the child was brought back to life, he sneezed seven times. God gave me the most wonderful revelation about deliverance through the story of the Shulamite woman's son.

Second Kings 4:35 says, "Elisha got up, walked back and forth across the room once, and then stretched himself out again on the child. This time the boy sneezed seven times and opened his eyes!" Through this passage God showed me that sneezing is a sign of deliverance. In the natural it's one way the body removes foreign matter, and the same happens in the spirit. In the story the young boy had been delivered from the spirit of death along with the other spirits associated with death (demons always work in gangs; where you find one, you'll find others more wicked around it). His sneezing was a sign of his deliverance.

When leading a deliverance session in which I feel I need

to address the nose, I often encourage the person to breathe in and out through his nose. While he is inhaling and exhaling, I command the demons to leave through the exhale, and I command all demons attacking the person's discernment to cease in their plans. Usually the person starts releasing mucus out of his or her nose (which is usually a sign that the demon is leaving; mucus is the perfect vehicle for a demon to use to ride out of the body). Sometimes during deliverance people will feel mildly embarrassed and try to keep the mucus from coming out. But it is important that the mucus be released from the body, as the demon is leaving the body on the mucus. If the mucus is swallowed or sniffed back into the nose, the demons will be able to remain. (This is something I've learned from personal experience.)

I had a dream once where I saw a demon hiding in a curtain. It started to come toward me, still hiding behind the curtain, and when it came close enough I grabbed it by the throat and ordered it to leave. When the demon was on its way out the window, my wife walked in the room, and the demon nipped her nose, and she sneezed. When I woke up I knew the devil was trying to attack my wife's discernment and that she needed some deliverance in this area (which she readily agreed to receive). I prayed and commanded the attacks to stop, and my wife received her freedom!

THE ANUS

The anus is an exit. Mark 7:18–19 (KJV) says:

> And he saith unto them, Are ye so without under-
> standing also? Do ye not perceive, that whatsoever
> thing from without entereth into the man, it cannot

> defile him; because it entereth not into his heart, but
> into the belly, and goeth out into the draught, purg-
> ing all meats?

There is no other purpose for this part of the body than to rid the body of waste. Demons know this and are always looking for way to abuse this body part through sexual exploitation, making it an entry instead of only an exit. Using the anus as an entry is an abomination. When conducting deliverance on those struggling with homosexuality, you must target prayer toward this exit to remove all demonic spirits lurking there.

Decree freedom in this body part by saying this prayer out loud:

> *Holy Spirit, every part of my body has been made
> by Your hands and is sacred ground, even the parts
> used for releasing waste. I repent for using this area
> to _____.* [Repent of whatever the Holy
> Spirit reveals; being specific targets the root.]
>
> *Lord Jesus, I ask You to sever every curse over this
> area. I renounce every demon hiding in this part of
> my anatomy. By the authority of Your name, I com-
> mand every demon to leave my body now. I declare
> this area cleansed by the blood of Jesus and now
> dedicated to God and to be used only for its original
> purpose. In Jesus's name, amen!* [Or you can con-
> tinue praying as the Holy Spirit guides you.]

THE GENITALS

The male genitals function as an exit. Their primary purpose is to release toxins and to release seed. Scripture outlines no other role for this body part. A distortion of this body part can be seen in homosexual activity, which is considered an abomination. When someone who is struggling with homosexuality is seeking deliverance, prayer must be targeted against the demons that abuse this particular body part. If not, the demons dwelling in this area will cause the person to desire homosexual activity again. And those struggling with fornication shouldn't just repent of the sin but also remove the demons hiding in those areas of the body that have been used as instruments of unrighteousness.

Unlike with males, the female genitals have a dual purpose as both an entrance and an exit. Females both receive the male seed and deliver babies. This area of the body is also used to release toxins. This is the area that demons have attacked the most through the ages. Barrenness is still a huge problem for many women. The demons that attack this area do so with aggression, because the devil hates it when women bring forth new life. He hates it when things are birthed in the spirit as well. If you find no biological reason you aren't able to conceive or if you're not birthing new things in the spirit, there may be a demon at work! Target your prayers toward the womb and rebuke whatever demonic entities are hiding there.

Use the following prayer starter to decree freedom in this part of the body. Adapt it as needed to address specific issues:

> Heavenly Father, by Your hands You fashioned the parts of my body that are private and ordained them to be used to honor You.
>
> Holy Spirit, I ask that You search this area of my body and remove every demon that is hiding in the secret places. I command them to leave right now in the name of Jesus. Holy Spirit, sanctify this part of my body and keep it holy. Let it be used only according to Your will and purpose. In Jesus's name, amen. [Or you can continue praying as the Holy Spirit guides you.]

THE SKIN

The skin functions as both an entrance and an exit (often serving as a secret passage for demons to go in and out of the body). This part of the body also plays a major role as a carrier of the glory of God. We see this in Exodus 34:29 (ESV):

> When Moses came down from Mount Sinai, with the two tablets of the testimony in his hand as he came down from the mountain, Moses did not know that the skin of his face shone because he had been talking with God.

Most of us breeze through this story and see Moses as a man who carried the glory after spending time in prayer. But the truth is, this account suggests that the glory of God can actually rest on a person's skin.

In the New Testament the apostles had spent so much time with Jesus that their skin reflected this same glory. In Acts 4:13 when the council members saw the courage of Peter and John and realized that they were unschooled, ordinary men, they were astonished and "they recognized that they had been with Jesus" (ESV). I believe they knew the men had been with Jesus because they saw the glory of God radiating from their skin. In another portion of Scripture Stephen is about to get stoned by the Jewish leaders. The Bible says when they looked at him, they saw that his face shone like that of an angel (Acts 6:15).

The same is true in the opposite. Demonic spirits can also rest on people's skin. Sometimes people carry a darkness on their faces that is extremely noticeable. Or their facial features may contort and take on an animallike quality through supernatural means. Deliverance from demons hiding in the skin can be seen in the life of Naaman, who had a skin disease called leprosy. The prophet Elisha told him to dip in the Jordan River seven times, and his skin disease would be healed. Upon Naaman's seventh dip, his skin became new like a baby's. This is a powerful depiction of deliverance in the skin; the Lord removed all demonic contamination and made Naaman's skin brand-new. (Read chapters 13 and 14 of the Book of Leviticus to learn more about skin diseases.) In addition, when we sweat, our bodies are removing toxins through the skin, and this is also a way demons may come out. (But you are not being delivered every time you sweat!)

Decree freedom in this part of the body by saying this prayer out loud:

> Jehovah Rapha, You're my healer! You're my strong tower. You're my Creator. My body was made for You, and You covered it with skin to protect it. You didn't create my body to be irritated, contaminated,

> *or infected. I order every demon hiding within the cells of my skin to leave me now in Jesus's name. I command every demon of _____ (insert the names of skin diseases or anything the Holy Spirit reveals) to release my skin now in Jesus's name. I decree that my skin is rejuvenated, brand-new, and healed now in the name of the Lord Jesus Christ. Amen!* [Or you can continue praying as the Holy Spirit guides you.]

CUTTING AWAY THE OLD

I want to close this chapter by talking about two parts of the body that are mentioned in Deuteronomy 21:11–13:

> And suppose you see among the captives a beautiful woman, and you are attracted to her and want to marry her. If this happens, you may take her to your home, where she must shave her head, cut her nails, and change the clothes she was wearing when she was captured.

The cutting of the hair and nails in Deuteronomy 21 represented the cutting away of the old lifestyle. When a woman from outside the camp wanted to marry an Israelite, she had to cut off her hair and nails, symbolizing the breaking off of every dead weight and removal of the old.

Our hair and nails are exits that represent that which is dead being removed from the body to make room for that which is new. I believe they serve as a model for daily deliverance. Just as our hair and nails shed daily, I believe we should pray daily for God to search our temples and bring deliverance in every area that we have not fully committed to Him.

Jesus said in the model for prayer, "And lead us not into temptation, but deliver us from the evil one" (Matt. 6:13, NIV). Most people think of temptation as something outside our lives that causes us to sin. But we can be tempted by internal desires coming from areas of our lives that aren't completely submitted to God. These are the areas where demons love to hide. By asking God to cleanse our temples each day, we keep from giving place to the devil (Eph. 4:27) and create room for God to do something new in and through us.

I encourage you to use this prayer as a prompt to ask God daily to deliver you from any demons hiding in unsurrendered areas of your life:

> Heavenly Father, I come to You today asking You to lead me not into temptation but to deliver me from the evil one. Search my temple and uncover any demons hiding in my life. Reveal any areas that I have not fully surrendered to You. [Address any spirits the Holy Spirit shows you, repenting of whatever actions gave them legal access, renouncing them out loud, and releasing blessing in their place.] I choose today to serve You with my whole heart. Thank You, Lord, for setting me free! In Jesus's name, amen. [Or you can continue praying as the Holy Spirit guides you.]

Now that we have examined the common entrances and exits, we will discuss the body parts that can easily be overlooked as areas of demonic habitation.

CHAPTER 5

RECOGNIZING OTHER
KEY DEMONIC TARGETS

*Then will I sprinkle clean water upon you, and
ye shall be clean: from all your filthiness, and
from all your idols, will I cleanse you.*
—EZEKIEL 36:25, KJV

IN THE PENTATEUCH (the first five books of the Bible),
especially in the Books of Leviticus and Numbers, we find
many references to removing certain body parts during animal sacrifices and presenting them as a separate offering
to God. For many years I overlooked such verses, assum-
ing those passages were outlining a requirement of the Law
and nothing more. But as I looked further into what I call
"deeper deliverance," I began to hear the Holy Spirit whisper
in my ear that I needed to pay closer attention to parts of the
body that are often overlooked.

In this chapter we will look at several more body parts
demons frequently target that are not necessarily entrances
or exits. Though there may be some minor overlap, I have
singled out these body parts because they have come up
often enough during deliverance sessions that I believe they
warrant special attention.

THE TONGUE

Although the tongue is part of the mouth area, I wanted to address it separately because the Bible has a great deal to say about this part of the body. There's even a whole chapter in the Book of James dedicated to it (James 3). The Bible says all of hell is set on fire by the tongue (James 3:6), therefore making it a lethal body part. The demons attached to the tongue manifest themselves in gossip, homosexuality and lesbianism (which both involve oral sex), lying, cursing, boasting, exaggerating, filthy talk, negative talk, ghetto street talk, the desire to wear tongue rings, backbiting, and the like.

An unrestrained tongue is a demonic playground because demons love to talk, especially during deliverance sessions. They will make it seem as though the person needs to share past experiences or to have someone listen to him. Such tactics are an attempt to get the minister to function more as a counselor (demons enjoy counseling sessions) rather than in the boldness of kingdom deliverance. I repeat: demons love to speak. So do people who spent most of their lives feeling voiceless and now seek to manipulate others through their words.

On one occasion I was called into my office and asked to conduct a deliverance session on someone who wanted to be free from homosexuality. This person happens to be a mature Christian with ministry experience. I reluctantly agreed, as homosexuality has proven to be a tough demon to handle. In addition to casting out demons, there must be mind renewal, counseling, and personal discipline on the part of the person seeking freedom. From the beginning of the session, it was obvious that this case was different, as I felt an unusual measure of wisdom to target my deliverance prayers with more precision.

I began to direct my attention to the tongue and call out demons associated with oral sex and other inappropriate uses of the tongue. Immediately there was a demonic manifestation, as the demon wasn't expecting there to be such targeted deliverance prayer. (Demons are used to hearing rote deliverance prayers and are often unmoved by them.) As the session continued, I became more detailed in my prayers focusing on the tongue.

I quoted Isaiah 6:6–7, using it as a basis for purging the person's tongue and cleansing it from demonic activity: "Then one of the seraphim flew to me with a burning coal he had taken from the altar with a pair of tongs. He touched my lips with it and said, 'See, this coal has touched your lips. Now your guilt is removed, and your sins are forgiven.'"

After a forty-minute session there was a powerful breakthrough, and the demon of homosexuality was dismantled. The power of the Holy Spirit is amazing to do targeted deliverance and dig deep to find the demons attaching themselves to a person's body parts.

Let me share with you another story to drive this point home. Several years ago a woman used to visit our church with her family. They were all new to church, and she seemed to enjoy coming, but she was never able to make a full commitment to Christ. I engaged this woman in conversation a couple times, but each time I had a hard time communicating effectively, as she was completely unchurched and her language was 100 percent street. Her communication was so heavily saturated with slang and broken English that I couldn't understand her. Each time we spoke, I walked away more confused as to why she couldn't turn off the slang and just have a regular conversation for two minutes.

After about two months I saw this sister one Sunday, and when she opened her mouth to respond to my greeting, I saw that she was wearing a tongue ring. I immediately discerned that a demon was attached to the tongue ring and that her tongue was a slave to that demon. Unfortunately even after many years the young lady still hasn't made a full commitment to Christ, but we are believing God for her salvation. In God's time we believe the Holy Spirit will grip her life, she will renounce her ways, and her tongue will be used to speak the oracles of God.

But for now the woman's tongue ring symbolizes the fact that she has yielded that area of her life to a demonic spirit. Any time a person, even a believer, submits his tongue to the will of the enemy, demonic contamination can occur and the potential becomes high that the body part will be used as an instrument of unrighteousness. The longer a person yields his tongue to darkness, the more the enemy will manipulate that body part and the person will eventually develop an inordinate desire to fulfill the lusts of the flesh. Again, this is why we target the tongue when praying for those seeking to be set free from homosexuality.

If the person is to experience freedom, the demonic spirit must be removed from that body part and the person must yield himself fully to God. As Colossians 3:5–6 says, "Mortify therefore your members which are upon the earth; fornication, uncleanness, inordinate affection, evil concupiscence, and covetousness, which is idolatry: For which things' sake the wrath of God cometh on the children of disobedience" (KJV).

Decree freedom in this part of the body by saying this prayer out loud:

> *Heavenly Father, Your Word says life and death are in the power of my tongue. Please forgive me for using my mouth in ways that don't glorify You. I renounce all corrupt communication, every form of evil speech, and all sinful acts I have committed with my tongue* [be specific as the Holy Spirit leads]. *I surrender my tongue to You and declare that my words will be used to edify. From this moment forth may my speech be always with grace, seasoned with salt. I decree that my words will be used to edify and build Your kingdom, not for gossip, backbiting, or any other form of negative talk. In Jesus's name, amen.* [Or you can continue praying as the Holy Spirit guides you.]

THE BONES

The bones are a less explored body part for deliverance. In fact, I can recall only one or two occasions when I had to expel a demon from the bones. But the Bible does speak of bones being full of sin in Job 20:11, "His bones are full of the sin of his youth, which shall lie down with him in the dust" (KJV).

The bones are an area that needs more investigation because demons don't actually dwell in the bones but in the marrow, where a person's DNA is stored. Spiritually the bones are where all information, both good and bad, is kept.

Job 20:11 said the man's bones were "full of the sin of his youth." This points to the bones as a storage room for all of a person's "files," including significant moments and memories.

Is it possible for bones to house demonic spirits? When you consider that the bones are nourished and replenished with blood that circulates through the human body and that blood carries information, I would say yes, it is possible for the bones to house a demon. During an intense time of personal attack because of the prophetic words the Lord had given him to speak, the prophet Jeremiah found himself at the point of giving up. He actually did give up, but in his moment of despair he was encouraged by the word of God that was like a *fire in his bones*: "But if I say I'll never mention the LORD or speak in his name, his word burns in my heart like a fire. It's like a fire in my bones! I am worn out trying to hold it in! I can't do it!" (Jer. 20:9).

The Bible speaks of two demons that are associated with the bones: envy and silence. Proverbs 27:4 says this about envy: "Wrath is cruel, and anger is outrageous; but who is able to stand before envy?" (KJV). Envy is a fierce enemy that desires what its neighbor possesses. It removes our happiness at seeing those around us blessed and secretly desires for them to not have something because we don't have that thing. After a prolonged period of not allowing the Holy Spirit to address the envy in our hearts, it begins to corrupt the bones. Most human problems that revolve around the bones are due to envy. Proverbs 14:30 says, "A sound heart is the life of the flesh: but envy the rottenness of the bones" (KJV).

Another way demons gain entry to our bones is when we

remain silent about things that hurt us deeply and don't process them correctly. The Bible says that when we are offended, we are to discuss the matter and, if possible, find solutions to resolve it. The enemy wants you silent! He desires for you to take all the hits and never come to terms with what happened or confront the person who offended you. We say we don't want anyone in our business, but God created us as speaking spirits, and communication is a vital part of our human experience. Saying something closes the door to the enemy, but silence opens it wide. Psalm 32:3 says, "When I kept silence, my bones waxed old through my roaring all the day long" (KJV).

Other signs of demonic activity in the bones are bitterness, confusion, being consistently stuck in life, and sickness. The way to cleanse the bones is to decree the fear of the Lord. Proverbs 3:7–8 says, "Don't be impressed with your own wisdom. Instead, fear the LORD and turn away from evil. Then you will have healing for your body and strength for your bones."

Use the following prayer to decree the fear of the Lord over your bones right now:

> *Father, in the name of Jesus, I stand on Your Word and declare that my bones are strong and in good health. I command blessing over every part of my skeletal system. I decree that all information stored in my bones be purged by the blood of Jesus, and I order every demon hiding in my bones to come out now in Jesus's name. Holy Spirit, I release Your presence over my bones. I saturate my bones with new things, new levels, new fire, new mantles, and new*

assignments. In Jesus's name, amen. [Or you can continue praying as the Holy Spirit guides you.]

THE BACK

I know the back is generally made up of bones, but I want to address this part of the body separately because of a reference to it in Luke 13 when Jesus healed the woman with the spirit of infirmity.

> And he was teaching in one of the synagogues on the sabbath. And, behold, there was a woman which had a spirit of infirmity eighteen years, and was bowed together, and could in no wise lift up herself. And when Jesus saw her, he called her to him, and said unto her, Woman, thou art loosed from thine infirmity. And he laid his hands on her: and immediately she was made straight, and glorified God.
>
> —LUKE 13:10–13, KJV

Jesus Himself confirmed that this woman was being afflicted for eighteen years by a demon of infirmity that was affecting her back. In addition to showing how a demon can manifest in a body part, this story also reveals that demons have assignments. This demon is called a "spirit of infirmity," meaning this demon had an assignment to bring sickness, and it focused its efforts on her back. This demon was so effective that it operated for eighteen years undisturbed until the great Deliverer showed up. Jesus exposed its works and loosed the woman from the demon.

If you are experiencing sickness or pain in your back, lay your hands on that part of your body and say this prayer:

> I command every spirit of infirmity dwelling in
> my back to come out in Jesus's name. I order you
> to remove all traces of your work and ways in my
> back. Wherever you're lodging in my back, I com-
> mand you to find your exit and leave me now in the
> name of Jesus. I decree God's glory to be unleashed
> upon my body in the back area, and I order my back
> to be straight and whole now in Jesus's name. Amen.

[Or you can continue praying as the Holy Spirit
guides you.]

THE FEET, TOES, AND THUMBS

"I felt a demon come out of my foot" is what a person told me
after I preached at a deliverance conference. It was the first
time anyone ever told me that, so it took me a couple minutes to process it through my "error" filters. But the more I
pondered it, the more it became apparent that the feet are
also a place where demons can dwell. Romans 3:15 talks
about people whose feet "are swift to shed blood" (NIV). The
word *swift* implies that they are quick and eager, and the text
says "their feet" were swift, not the people!

That verse isn't denying that those individuals were
responsible for their actions. But it acknowledges, as the
apostle Paul did, that sin can dwell within our "members,"
or our body parts (Rom. 7:23, KJV). Sometimes a person's
actions aren't just a work of the flesh. As I mentioned previously, there are times when a demon hiding in a part of the
body will cause the person's predisposition toward a particular sin to increase.

I've seen this firsthand when dealing with spirits of lust.

Often when I command the demon of lust to leave the person's hands, the individual will be set free. So I'm open to the idea that a demon could be living in a foot, a big toe, or a finger. As matter of fact, in the Book of Exodus we find God focusing Moses's attention on his nephews' big toes.

> Next Moses presented Aaron's sons and applied some
> of the blood to the lobes of their right ears, the thumbs
> of their right hands, and the big toes of their right feet.
> He then splattered the rest of the blood against all
> sides of the altar.
> —LEVITICUS 8:24

Why would God want there to be a purging of these specific body parts? They all represent a part of the body we don't usually investigate for demonic contamination. Demons hide in these areas like an armed robber living in plain sight on the last city street at the farthest point, where no one is looking for them. The big toes and thumbs represent the parts of your body that are at the farthest points of your body—the perfect place for demons to hide!

Signs and symptoms of demonic activity in the feet, toes, and thumbs include extreme cases of arthritis (extreme illnesses that confound doctors may be caused by demons), nerve damage with no root cause, and an inability to walk with no root cause.

Many years ago I encountered a believer God had called to be a powerful intercessor. This man had a grace to impart strength to others, but somewhere along the line he was offended by his pastor and began to criticize him and the local church. Ultimately he joined another church. But after some time at this new church, this man again became offended at the pastors and left that church as well. In his new church he became offended yet again, and as usual began to publicly criticize the church, but this time this man was smitten with a disease in his feet. The doctors couldn't find the root of the problem, and to this day he is unable to walk.

I happened to run into him many years after we first met, and I encouraged him to forgive his offenders because offense, bitterness, and unforgiveness were at the root of his inability to walk. He looked at me and screamed, "No!" and then told his attendant to take him home. It was sad to see this man reject healing because of his inability to let go of offense.

The man who was at the pool of Bethesda in John 5 had been there for thirty-eight years. When Jesus healed him, He gave him this strong warning: "Behold, thou art made whole: sin no more, lest a worse thing come unto thee" (John 5:14, KJV). The Bible is letting us know that the root cause of this man's thirty-eight-year lameness was sins of his heart.

It's not worth having your feet cursed (or any other part of your body) because you refuse to walk in forgiveness. Forgive and let it go now. Walk in the freedom Christ purchased for you on the cross when He said, "Father, forgive them; for they know not what they do" (Luke 23:34, KJV).

To break the assignment of spirits attached to these body parts, release this prayer over yourself:

> *With my authority in Christ, I declare blessings over the parts of my body that are the least inspected. Holy Spirit, go to those areas least explored, the areas I've overlooked. I decree that my hands are*

blessed. I decree that my feet are blessed now in Jesus's name. I command every demon living in the ulterior regions of my heart, mind, soul, and body to leave me now in Jesus's name. Unclean spirit, find your exit out of my body now in Jesus's name! Amen. [Or you can continue praying as the Holy Spirit guides you.]

THE FACE

We discussed the skin in the last chapter, but during many of the deliverance sessions we've conducted, both my staff and I have seen what can only be described as demons hiding in the face. There's often a moment when the face of the person sitting in front of us goes through a demonic contortion. The subject of deliverance is still considered taboo in many denominations, so there hasn't been enough light shed on this topic, but those of us who actually do deliverance have seen this kind of demonic contortion with our own eyes.

I'm reminded of a deliverance session once when a woman's face contorted to look like that of a gorilla. Her features became very gorilla-like, and her hands began to ball into fists. We immediately knew the demon of anger and rage was very upset that it had been exposed and was making a last-ditch effort to intimidate. (When demons show displays of power, such tactics are designed to put the deliverance minister in fear rather than trusting in God.) Within ten minutes the power of God showed up, and we were able to help this woman.

The Bible says in Proverbs 15:13 that "a happy heart makes the face cheerful, but heartache crushes the spirit" (NIV).

This verse lets us know that the face reveals what's going on in the heart. Demons of anger, rage, fear, and worry can be seen on their victims' faces. Another group of demons that can be seen on the face are the homosexual and lesbian demons. These demons cause their victims to take on the characteristics of the opposite sex. As much as someone may try to mask it, the demons attached to gender confusion are not hiding their activity. It's imperative when getting set free from homosexuality that the deliverance minister targets the face to remove any residue still lingering there.

To cleanse your face of any demonic activity, pray this out loud:

> *Holy Spirit, my face belongs to You to reflect Your presence in my life. I command every demon hiding in my face—in or on my nasal cavities, cheekbones, nostrils, eyebrows, or forehead—to leave now. Come out now and take with you all traces of your presence in Jesus's name. Spirit of God, come upon me now and rest on my face as the dove rested on Jesus when He was baptized. Let my face reflect Your glory. In Jesus's name, amen.* [Or you can continue praying as the Holy Spirit guides you.]

BE CLEANSED INSIDE AND OUT

In Exodus 29:17–18 God said, "And thou shalt cut the ram in pieces, and wash the inwards of him, and his legs, and put them unto his pieces, and unto his head. And thou shalt burn the whole ram upon the altar: it is a burnt offering unto the LORD: it is a sweet savour, an offering made by fire unto the LORD" (KJV). I've often read this passage and wondered exactly why God placed so much emphasis on the cleaning of the inward parts (internal organs).

I believe it's because the Lord wants us to be clean inside and out. He doesn't want there to be areas of our lives that are not surrendered to the Holy Spirit. The sacrifice referenced in Exodus 29:17–18 required that the inward parts be cleansed and presented as a burnt offering. In the New Testament we see that the Lord still desires that we are cleansed in our inward parts. Second Corinthians 7:1 says, "Dearly beloved, let us cleanse ourselves from all filthiness of the flesh and spirit, perfecting holiness in the fear of God" (KJV).

Sadly, due to irresponsibility, it is often the case that our hearts belong to Jesus but our bodies have become a habitation for demonic contamination. God wants to inhabit every part of us, not just our hearts. He says in Ezekiel 36:25, "Then will I sprinkle clean water upon you, and ye shall be clean: from all your filthiness, and from all your idols, will I cleanse you" (KJV). This is done through the ministry of deliverance.

To give the Holy Spirit control over every part of your life, including your body parts, declare this prayer out loud now:

> Lord Jesus, my heart belongs to You, my body belongs to You, my mind belongs to You, my emotions belong to You, and all the hidden parts of my heart belong to You. I humbly ask You to go into the innermost parts of my life and remove every demon. I command every demon hiding deep within me to expose itself and come out of my body now in Jesus's name.

Holy Spirit, I release Your glory all over my body, and may every room of my life be saturated with Your renovating presence, in Jesus's name. Amen. [Or you can continue praying as the Holy Spirit guides you.]

CHAPTER 6

GOING DEEPER IN DELIVERANCE

Then he brought me to the door of the Temple courtyard, where I could see a hole in the wall. He said to me, "Now, son of man, dig into the wall." So I dug into the wall and found a hidden doorway. "Go in," he said.... Then the LORD said to me, "Son of man, have you seen what the leaders of Israel are doing with their idols in dark rooms?"
—EZEKIEL 8:7–9, 12

IN RECENT YEARS a cry has gone out for a deeper level of deliverance. So many people have tried every method they know to gain freedom but have seen little or no change. As I mentioned previously, some methods of deliverance are outdated and ineffective, as the kingdom of darkness has taken its work deeper inside the "house." For this reason, the body of Christ needs more precise deliverance strategies that address bondage on microscopic levels.

We need the Holy Spirit to bring new insight and to spotlight areas the church has overlooked when conducting deliverance. In the previous two chapters we looked at how to expel demons hiding in parts of the body. But as we saw in chapter 2, demons also hide in "rooms" in a person's soul. But how do we discover these demons?

In Ezekiel 8 God showed the prophet a hole in the wall.

Then He commanded Ezekiel to dig into the wall because He wanted him to discover a hidden doorway. Perhaps lately you have been sensing the Holy Spirit highlighting areas in your life that He wants you to dig into to discover the root issue. Don't ignore it. That is a divine invitation to freedom!

Finding the root of a problem is not an easy task, especially when your tools for investigation are ineffective. It's like you're trying to conduct a forensic investigation with only a magnifying glass. Plus, it's hard to enter a room that you don't know exists because it's hidden behind an artificial wall.

I'm alarmed when I read Ezekiel 8 and see that if had God not highlighted the hole in the wall, Ezekiel never would have noticed it. The mere thought that there could be an area in my heart that I'm unaware of where demons function without resistance *frightens me*, and it should frighten you too.

This thought caused me to spend countless hours praying and spending time with the Holy Spirit, asking Him to reveal anything that was hidden in my life. King David was aware of these hidden areas when he said in Psalm 19:12, "How can I know all the sins lurking in my heart? Cleanse me from these *hidden* faults" (emphasis added).

The Holy Spirit desires that the church go deeper in deliverance, and I believe Ezekiel 8 shows us how.

THE THREE STEPS

In the passage from Ezekiel 8 quoted at the opening of this chapter, the prophet Ezekiel did three things that serve as a model for going deeper in deliverance.

1. He saw the signs (gained insight).

2. He dug through the wall (searched out the spirit).

3. He went inside the room (confronted the enemy).

Let's look at each one.

See beyond sight

Had God not led Ezekiel to the wall with the hole in it, the prophet may have walked by it without ever realizing there was a room hidden behind it. That wall likely was not there when the house was first built, but it was placed there to conceal what was going on in secret. When it comes to deliverance, the biggest problem isn't your vision, it's your insight. Insight is the ability to see deeper into a thing, to be able to discern.

You can be a very prophetic person or even walk in the office of a prophet and still remain completely ignorant of what's happening in hidden rooms. Throughout my years in ministry I have heard only a few people really teach in-depth on the need to have insight when ministering deliverance. Yet insight is the very thing the apostle Paul prayed the Ephesian church would receive:

> Ever since I first heard of your strong faith in the Lord Jesus and your love for God's people everywhere, I have not stopped thanking God for you. I pray for you constantly, asking God, the glorious Father of our Lord Jesus Christ, to give you spiritual wisdom

and *insight* so that you might grow in your knowledge
of God.
—EPHESIANS 1:15–17, EMPHASIS ADDED

When God commanded Ezekiel to look at the wall, He
was challenging his sight! I imagine Ezekiel thought he was
just seeing a wall, nothing special about it. But when God
gave him *insight*, he noticed a hole in the wall. The average
believer seeking deliverance has failed to notice the small
signs the Holy Spirit has been trying to point out. As you
read this, the Holy Spirit is saying, "Ask Me for insight, and
I will show you what's right in front of your face." If you're
a deliverance minister, the Holy Spirit is saying, *"Pay attention."* If something seems off during a deliverance session,
follow that trail, no matter how small. What has made me
effective in deliverance ministry is that I pay attention to
the small things.

Once you start to pay attention, you will notice things
you hadn't seen before, which leads to the second truth we
can learn from Ezekiel's actions. If you see a hole, *dig!*

Start digging

Once Ezekiel saw the hole, he was commanded to dig.
Oh, how we hate to dig. It's time-consuming, but truthfully
if you're not willing to roll up your sleeves and dig and dig
and dig to find the root issue, then you're not serious about
deeper deliverance. The Bible doesn't say how long Ezekiel
was digging, but we know it took time because he was digging in a wall, not in the ground. There is a huge difference
between walls and ground. Digging through a wall requires
a lot more effort and stronger tools.

Digging through the wall requires us to ask the tough questions about our family's history. It requires us to fast and pray and bombard heaven to reveal what we're overlooking. Digging through the wall requires us to do some soul searching so we can dismantle the wall brick by brick until all the debris is gone and what's been hidden is brought into the light.

You can get to the root of the problem if you take the time to dig! Hebrews 11:6 declares that God rewards "those who diligently seek Him" (MEV). There is a reward awaiting those who make it their business to go to the lengths necessary to get free. God responds to groaning. Freedom is your inheritance in Christ. It's what Jesus came to earth to give freely to those willing to receive it. First John 3:8 tells us that "for this purpose the Son of God was manifested, that he might destroy the works of the devil" (KJV).

Digging also disturbs what's been living in undisturbed areas. There may be demonic influences in our lives that aren't as severe as our main issues but have joined in for the ride. When our digging causes a disruption, there will be minor manifestations of resistance. Don't be alarmed. These are demonic tactics to get you to stop digging. Whatever you do, don't stop digging because all types of creatures that live in the "walls" will be forced to come out.

Demons hate investigation, and they will discourage it with weariness, personal attack, discouragement, and more. When none of those things stops you from digging, the snakes living in old walls will begin to manifest and bite, as Ecclesiastes 10:8–9 says:

> When you dig a well, you might fall in. When you
> demolish an old wall, you could be bitten by a snake.
> When you work in a quarry, stones might fall and
> crush you.

Demons love mediocrity and apathy. They thrive off believers having no passion to pursue freedom. But when the true kingdom of God has arrived, it will interfere with the kingdom of darkness. It will aggressively confront what has remained hidden in the rooms for years.

Walk inside the room

The final step Ezekiel took was that he entered the room and began to see the root causes of every ailment affecting the true worship of Yahweh in the temple. These ninety side rooms that King Solomon built to serve as storage rooms, dressing rooms, kitchens, and so on, had become resting places for unclean spirits and all sorts of abominations. When Ezekiel entered the rooms God led him to, he found images painted on the wall (which represent demonic memories) and the seventy elders burning incense to false gods. In another area of the temple a group of women were weeping for the false god Tammuz.

The prophet was given insight into the contaminations in these rooms King Solomon built. He was being shown areas deep inside the temple where demonic spirits were functioning undetected. God Himself was giving Ezekiel access to what really was going on in the hearts of the elders of Israel during the time of the Babylonian captivity. The finished work of Christ on the cross has given the New Testament believer that same access to the rooms of our temples. We have been given the keys of the kingdom to access all that God has given us. (See Matthew 16:19.)

To help you better understand this revelation, let me give you an example from a time when I had the privilege of using these keys during a deliverance session. After service one Sunday my wife and I were cornered in the front of the church by a woman seeking a third deliverance session. We agreed to help her, as she was an active member of our church and had been marvelously delivered from life on the street. This woman was living for the Lord, but she came from a rough, street background and was having a hard time changing old habits. During the session I asked the Holy Spirit to reveal to me what was at the root of her current problem. God gave me a mini-vision, and as clear as day I saw an old wooden door.

In front of the door I saw the person's mother saying hurtful words of rejection. Behind the door was a room called "Abortion." As soon as I asked the woman if "abortion" meant anything to her, she burst out crying, as she had undergone five abortions that she'd kept secret for years. I proceeded to open the door to the "daughter room" (something I will discuss in the next chapter) and began commanding every unclean spirit of rejection and abortion to come out. By the power of Jesus's name they all came out, and this woman was delivered from the demons hiding in this room in her soul as well as the problem for which she came to us for deliverance.

Different Keys to Different Rooms

Having the keys to the kingdom is an awesome privilege. But while it ensures your authority and access to the rooms, it doesn't guarantee that you'll have the wisdom to know which keys open which doors. Not knowing how to use the keys is just as ineffective in deliverance ministry as not knowing the rooms even exist. When dealing with tough cases and resistant demons, most deliverance ministers will stand in front of a door and just try key after key until they find the right one. Not knowing how to utilize the right key during deliverance is like a prosecutor not knowing which charges to file against the perpetrator of a crime. Without the right charge, the prosecutor will have a very hard time convicting a criminal, and without the right key, you'll have a very hard time removing resistant demons.

Demons thrive off ignorance and will make a deliverance session last for hours, like a guilty defendant taking his case to trial and letting it drag on for months. Guessing which key opens the door is a waste of valuable time. One of the roles of the Holy Spirit is to guide us into all truth, and He will show us which key to use. Deliverance requires a total dependence on the Holy Spirit to reveal which key will open the prison doors and set the captive free.

In the next chapter we are going to look at several rooms that exist in the human soul, their primary functions, and then how to cleanse them of any demonic activity.

CHAPTER 7

KEY ROOMS TO TARGET FOR DELIVERANCE

*Then the man told me, "These rooms that overlook
the Temple from the north and south are holy. Here
the priests who offer sacrifices to the LORD will eat
the most holy offerings. And because these rooms are
holy, they will be used to store the sacred offerings.*
—EZEKIEL 42:13

WHENEVER I AM leading someone through deliverance, there are certain key rooms that I almost always target to ensure there are no demons hiding in them. In this chapter we are going to look at those rooms, but before we dive into that, I want to share two important truths about the rooms in our souls.

First, Ezekiel 42:13, quoted at the beginning of this chapter, indicates that the rooms in the temple were holy, and the same is true of the rooms in our souls. The rooms in our lives are holy because God made them. He made each area of our souls perfectly to be used for His purposes. But just as it was in Ezekiel's day, the enemy sneaks in and contaminates the rooms in our lives. Only when we purge them can we begin to walk in God's original purpose and design for that area of our lives.

A second truth is revealed in 1 Kings 6:6:

> The complex was three stories high, the bottom floor
> being 7½ feet wide, the second floor 9 feet wide, and
> the top floor 10½ feet wide. The rooms were con-
> nected to the walls of the Temple by beams resting on
> ledges built out from the wall.

This verse indicates that each floor of the temple was a
different size, which suggests that each floor had a different
level of importance. Just as certain roles in your life are more
important than others, so are certain rooms in your heart
more important than others. For example, my name is Alexander Pagani, and I am a husband, father, son, pastor, US cit-
izen, Latino, and more. These roles are not all of me; they are
only part of me. My role as a father to my sons, Apollos and
Xavier, does not have the same level of importance as my
role as the senior pastor of He Is Risen Tabernacle (HIRT).
I'm both a father and a pastor, but one role is more important than the other. How I interact with my sons directly
affects how they will live their lives as they carry my last
name, but my role as senior pastor is lesser in comparison, as
I am a spiritual advisor to the congregation, not their father.
Both are very important but not *equally* important.

The more important the role (room), the more demons
will target it. If a man has children, one of the most significant roles he can function in is as an active father. This is
why there is such a lack of fathers and father figures today.
The father room has been the target of the devil since the
world began because it's a reflection of the eternal relationship between God the Father and His Son, Jesus Christ. In
almost all the deliverance sessions my wife and I have led
through the years, a father wound is at the root of most of

the problems people face. This is why I often start deliverance sessions in the "son" or "daughter" room. There's almost always a demonic manifestation if you start there!

For the remainder of this chapter I will look at several of the most important rooms in our lives and the demons that like hide within them. As you read about these rooms, please ask the Holy Spirit to reveal to you if there is any demonic attachment in these rooms (roles) in your life. If you are a deliverance worker, then learning about these rooms will help you identify potential demonic influence in those you're trying to help gain freedom. The prayers are written for those going through self-deliverance, but they can easily be adapted by a deliverance minister.

The list of rooms in this chapter is not exhaustive, but it will help give a basic understanding of how and which demons hide in certain areas of our lives. Though there is more for the Holy Spirit to reveal, what is included here will give you enough illumination to help light your path as you seek deliverance or pray for others.

ROOMS RELATED TO THE MALE GENDER

The Bible says in Genesis chapter 2 that God created mankind for the purpose of fellowship, to be His governing agent on the earth, to expand His kingdom and have dominion. And we were created with multiple roles inherent within us. Psalm 8:5 says, "What is man that you are mindful of him, and the son of man that you care for him? Yet you have made him a little lower than the heavenly beings and crowned him with glory and honor" (ESV). Men and women both are born with these God-given attributes. Our inherent nature is not far from that of angels, and deep within we carry God's glory (His divine attributes) and the honor that comes with it.

But God gave men unique roles and responsibilities that Satan and his cohorts spend most of their time trying to contaminate and distort. The Bible says men are called to be the head of the family, the high priest of the home, a source of provision for our families, representatives of God's kingdom, prophets, protectors, leaders, and much more. If any of these roles are dysfunctional, then it's time to dig deep and find out what's causing the malfunction. Almost always you will find the presence of an evil spirit. In this section I want to address three key rooms where demons like to hide to keep men from becoming who God created them to be.

The male room

The first role given to you at birth is your gender identification. This establishes all the rooms (roles) for every male on this earth. Inherent within every baby male is the capacity to be the head, high priest, provider, etc., of his home. Those roles are already assigned to him, and as he grows and matures, he is made aware of them and given the keys to govern the room (role).

Satan begins his assault on the male child as soon as he comes out of the womb. Revelation 12:4 says the dragon was waiting by the womb for the Christ child to be born to devour Him. What a powerful depiction of the kingdom of darkness's agenda against every male child born into the world. We are born in warfare. We breathed our first breath and had to fight to get our second.

Demons that attack this room start at birth and come in

through womb rejection, where the parents didn't plan to have a child or one of the parents wanted the opposite gender. Other spirits that occupy this room are demons of gender confusion, where from an early age the demon begins to suggest the child has an attraction to the same sex, especially if the person was raped or molested. If a boy grows up in a home with only the opposite gender, he may begin to mimic what he sees to be accepted. (I've seen this many times!)

Demons that are specifically sent to attack the male gender include rejection, sexual perversion, pride, homosexuality, rebellion, and succubus, just to name a few. When leading a man through deliverance, it is a good idea to begin the session by addressing the spirits that often reside in this room. You can invite the person to pray the following prayer:

> *Heavenly Father, I am Your son and You created me fearfully and wonderfully to be a male. You placed within me everything I need to become a man who honors You and fulfills Your plan for my life. Lord, bring to light anything in me that doesn't reflect Christlike manhood and any demons hiding in this room. I renounce every demon of _____ [name the demons the Holy Spirit reveals] on assignment in me, and I sever every generational curse of _____ [name the curses the Holy Spirit reveals]. I order every demon hiding in the male room to leave my body now in Jesus's name. Release over my life the strength and boldness to rise up and be the man You ordained me to be. In Jesus's name, amen.*

The husband room

Adam was a husband before he became a father, so being a father is not more important than being a husband. God gave Adam a helpmeet named Eve before He gave him his first child. Once the children come, too many couples put more focus on their kids than on their marriage. But God put marriage before children for a reason, and it should remain that way. The way Adam treated Eve and the kind of marriage they modeled impacted their children's outlook on male-female relationships, and the same is true today. It's important to me that my children see me enjoying a happy marriage with my wife, their mother, so I can pass that legacy on to them. I want them to see me loving my wife as Christ loves the church (Eph. 5:25–29).

Unlike with the son room or the male gender room, the husband room is for married men only. Demons spend a lot of time keeping the church focused on cleansing the father room to keep us from addressing the husband room because they know strong families are built on strong marriages. Most husbands battle demons of failure, fear of not being able to provide and secure a future for their families, and much more. Added to that is society's perception of men as ignorant and incompetent, and many men *believe this* about themselves! This lack of confidence is caused by a *demon*!

Sadly many men do struggle to be the head of the household and lead the family. Wives often pick up the slack, which causes their husbands to feel not needed (and the wives to feel resentment that their husbands are not being the high priest of the home!). When a husband feels underappreciated and overlooked by his wife, he becomes a breeding ground for demons! (Some women listen more quickly to their pastors than their own husbands.) Demons will invade this room and cause all kinds of chaos.

Symptoms of a demonic habitation in this room include apathy, procrastination, lack of motivation, laziness, bisexuality, and fantasizing. The tendency to retreat into a fantasy world is why many men are obsessed with video games well into their adulthood. Sometimes this fantasizing creeps into the marriage bed, causing the husband to fantasize about another woman—perhaps someone who honored him in some way—while he is being intimate with his wife.

If you're married and you can relate to what I've said, you need to clean out the husband room. Target your prayers to remove the demons of spousal rejection and the other issues connected to demonic habitation in this room. You can begin right now by saying this prayer out loud:

> Heavenly Father, I ask You to open the door to the room where You called me to be a husband to Your daughter. I'm asking that You begin the process of my deliverance in this area.
>
> Holy Spirit, bring to light any demons dwelling in this room. I order every demon hiding in this room to leave now in Jesus's name!
>
> I command the demon of _____ [name the demons the Holy Spirit reveals to you] to come out of my body now in Jesus's name. I order you to leave and take everything in the husband room that belongs to you, in Jesus's name!

> *Heavenly Father, I decree healing and restoration in this room and ask that You put everything in order! In Jesus's name, amen.*

The son room

There are many roles and many rooms we as men assume, but time will not allow me to address each one, so I want to focus on just one more: the son room. I chose this room because not every person reading this book is married or will ever be married, but every male is somebody's son! The devil works to occupy this room from birth, especially if the male grows up without a father figure. This child's sense of self-worth and identity is already distorted because he hasn't had a male in his life to serve as role model.

Most men today grow up without a dad, and a man without a father figure is too often ruled by unregulated desire. The demons in this room can manifest through abandonment, rejection, low self-worth, lack of enthusiasm, rebellion, anger, rage, a hard heart, a lack of affection, procrastination, laziness, quitting, and more. But of all the demons that attach themselves to this room, the one I most want to expose is the demon of "arrested development." This term refers to psychological development that is not complete. Another way to put it is that the person has aged in body but not in mind.

If there is any demon that needs to be confronted when taking a man through deliverance, it's this one. Many men have stopped aging mentally and are operating in a grown-up world with a childlike mind-set. As a result, they are living up to society's low expectations of them.

The apostle Paul addressed the issue of arrested development in his letter to the Corinthians. This church was the most anointed of all the congregations Paul planted, but they were the most immature. In 1 Corinthians 13 Paul said, "When I was a child, I spake as a child, I understood as a child, I thought as a child: but when I *became* a man, I put away childish things" (v. 11, KJV, emphasis added).

This verse is talking about deliverance. When Paul says he "put away childish things," he is referring to the moment when his old paradigm of immaturity was eradicated. A man is functioning with a childish paradigm when he gets angry over small things, or when he becomes confused when given too much information at once, or when he is unable to process through hard choices and make tough decisions. If you're male and you can identify with that I'm saying, you need deliverance in this area. Repeat this prayer after me and let's cleanse this room.

> *I come against any demons of arrested development hiding in the son room, causing me to manifest actions of rebellion, anger, and hard heart. I order these demons to come out of this room of my heart now in Jesus's name!*
>
> *Holy Spirit, I ask that You cleanse this room and put it back in order in Jesus's name!*
>
> *Heavenly Father, restore unto me the revelation and grace of sonship. You are my Father, and I want to walk in the reality of that truth for the rest of my life. In Jesus's name, amen.*

ROOMS RELATED TO THE FEMALE GENDER

Women are so important—and I don't think they fully understand just how significant they are. Of all God's creation, women stand alone. They are unique by design. God created the female to meet Adam's need for companionship and to be a helper to him. A woman is flesh of man's flesh and bone of man's bone, yet she is very different from him—so different that women became the object of angelic desire.

The Bible says in Genesis 6:2 that the sons of God saw that the daughters of men were beautiful and took them as wives. Why such a drastic breaking of rank to pursue another species? There was no other creature like them. The Bible refers to angels as masculine, and every angel that was named in Scripture has been male (Michael, Gabriel, Lucifer). Even the word translated "angel" in the Bible, *angelos*, is the masculine form of the term. So we have no reason to believe the angels had seen anything like women before.

Although it is debated whether all angels are male, it is safe to say that women have always been unique among God's creations. And as we saw with Eve in the Garden of Eden, Satan will often attack women first. I believe this is because women bring forth new life and because they have a powerful influence on men and the home. When demons attack women, many times they will go right for a woman's identity, which is why we must address demonic activity in the female room.

The female room

By birth women are created with a whole different skill set from men, which means the kingdom of darkness has to create a whole new strategy when it comes to dealing with women. Women are different because God gave women a different command than He gave men. The woman was given the important task of helping man fulfill his assignment on the earth. This is why the serpent did not focus his efforts on man, for man cannot do it alone. He needs a helper, so the serpent attacked the helper.

Still to this day he attacks the helpmeets with all the forces of hell. When Eve sinned after eating from the tree of the knowledge of good and evil, the consequences were swift and severe. One of the punishments given to women, aside from the pain of childbearing, can be found in Genesis 3:16 (emphasis added):

> Then he said to the woman, "I will sharpen the pain of your pregnancy, and in pain you will give birth. And you will *desire to control* your husband, but he will rule over you."

If there is one area where the devil attacks women, it is in the need to control people, things, circumstances, etc. The desire to be a controller is part of the curse, and the devil exploits it. This is why the spirit of Jezebel can be found more often in women than in men (though men can be Jezebels too), for the spirit of Jezebel manipulates to gain control.

The female room is the area of the heart where Jezebel spirits hide. You might think, "I just like to get things done and have things in order." But many times that type of behavior can be rooted in control.

If you feel control is an issue in your life, be honest and

repent. Let's begin the deliverance process right now. Say this prayer out loud and let's clean out the female room:

> *Heavenly Father, I'm Your special creation and the apple of Your eye, and I need deliverance in this room. I'm asking You to go into this room and turn on the all the lights and find the demons that are hiding.*
>
> *I command every demon in this room to leave me now! Rejection, lack of self-worth, loneliness, sadness, manipulation—leave my body now in Jesus's name.*
>
> *Holy Spirit, I declare Your glory over my life, over this room, and over my mind now in Jesus's name. Jesus, I ask You to clean this room and put every-thing I order. Thank You! Amen.*

The wife room

This room gets overlooked the most! So much time is spent helping women deal with the traumas of their past that the room dealing with their role as a wife is all but completely ignored. If a woman is married, she may have more damage in this area than in any other room.

There are three main reasons God places so much empha-sis on this role. The first is that in the beginning, the Godhead had a conversation about Adam's need for com-panionship and specifically created Eve to be a helpmeet for him. The second is that this helpmeet is a necessary vessel for the procreation of humankind. Last, the way a wife is treated by her husband has the ability to determine whether his prayers are answered or hindered.

Originally Adam found companionship in God alone. But God felt it wasn't good for man to be alone, so He created a helper who was "just right for him" (Gen. 2:18). Just as it is with men, Eve's role as a spouse came before her role as a parent. Eve was created as a wife first, then she became a mother. This is why if a woman is married, the wife room is one of the first areas I investigate during deliverance. Demons spend a lot of time wreaking havoc in this room, and they have systems in place to make sure the wife feels underappreciated, resentful, bitter, and overlooked by her husband. These issues have to be addressed.

We find this in the story of Jacob's wives and concubines. The women were in a bitter feud, trying to gain his attention and love, as we see in Genesis 29:34: "Then she became pregnant a third time and gave birth to another son. He was named Levi, for she said, 'Surely this time my husband will feel affection for me, since I have given him three sons!'" If you're married and you find it difficult to get delivered, you might need to place more emphasis on cleaning out the wife room and dealing with whatever may be lingering there.

In addition to being a helpmeet, women give birth to the next generation. Throughout the Bible, a high value is placed on fertility. It's because of a woman that the Son of God came into the earth to save humanity from our sins. Women are certainly not just "machines" made for procreation, but it can't be denied that God chose women to be the vehicles that carry powerful agents of change. They are the first to carry the weight of those who carry God's glory. This is another reason Satan attacks women—because he is afraid of what they carry on the inside!

Last, demons spend a lot of time trying to put wives at odds with their husbands because when the husband is at odds with his wife, the Bible says his prayers cannot be answered:

> In the same way, you husbands must give honor to your wives. Treat your wife with understanding as you live together. She may be weaker than you are, but she is your equal partner in God's gift of new life. Treat her as you should so your prayers will not be hindered.
>
> —1 PETER 3:7

The attacks a wife experiences are not always about hindering her but about deactivating her husband's power as the high priest of their home. Oh, how I wish wives would understand how the enemy manipulates situations. When a wife doesn't surround her husband with support, encouragement, words of affirmation, and the like, she plays into the devil's hands to create a wedge between her and her husband. If you find that as a wife you are filled will negativity and distrust and are constantly nitpicking and bickering, demons may have gained access to your wife room.

Let me give you an example. One afternoon I was contacted by the agent of a famous basketball player asking if I would see his wife for possible deliverance. I agreed and later that evening the wife showed up at the church. I immediately could tell she being tormented by demons, as she was nothing more than skin and bones. As the wife of a NBA celebrity, she would go weeks without seeing him as he traveled with his team. The unresolved conflict in the area of trust caused her to become extremely suspicious.

In her loneliness she dabbled in the occult by consulting a family spiritualist and opened wide the door for demons.

She was plagued by thoughts of suicide and a fear of dying. By the time she came to my office, her husband and friends didn't know what to do. In my conversations with her she expressed a lot of resentment toward her husband and his family. I realized the demons were attacking her role as wife. I targeted my prayers toward this room, and there was an immediate demonic manifestation. After about thirty minutes of helping her repent of not fully trusting in the Lord for answers and instead consulting a witch, she experienced breakthrough and relief from the demons that tormented her.

In addition to what has already been discussed, signs and symptoms of demonic activity in the wife room include rejection, feelings of ugliness and worthlessness, feeling overlooked, depression, and debilitating regret.

If you believe demonic spirits may have gained a foothold in the wife room, let's clean it out right now. Say this prayer out loud:

> *Heavenly Father, I ask You to open the door to the room where you called me to be a wife to Your son. I'm asking that You begin the process of my deliverance in this area.*
>
> *Holy Spirit, bring to light any demons dwelling in this room. I order every demon hiding in this room to leave now in Jesus's name! I command the demon of _____ [name the demons the Holy Spirit reveals to you] to come out of my body now in Jesus's name. I order you to leave and take everything in the wife room that belongs to you, in Jesus's name!*

> *Heavenly Father, I decree healing and restoration in this room and ask that You put everything in order! In Jesus's name, amen.*

The daughter room

Not every woman becomes a wife and not every woman becomes a mother, but every woman is a daughter. The Bible makes it clear that God wants to be our Father. Second Corinthians 6:17–18 says, "Therefore, come out from among unbelievers, and separate yourselves from them, says the LORD. Don't touch their filthy things, and I will welcome you. And I will be your Father, and you will be my sons and *daughters*, says the LORD Almighty" (emphasis added). The daughters of God are not second-class citizens. They have the same rights, privileges, and inheritance as the sons.

The desire to connect to a father figure dwells deep within the heart of every female, whether they know it or not. This is why the enemy spends most of his efforts trying to contaminate the daughter room by removing the father figures from young girls' lives.

The pain of fatherlessness doesn't just affect men. Fathers provide identity, self-worth, direction, and protection—all the building blocks that are needed for a girl to become a healthy and virtuous woman with a strong sense of self-worth. A father's words of affirmation can help his daughter realize her self-worth, but when that father figure is removed, demonic spirits will try to get girls to look for affirmation outside their home, even at an early age.

The demons in this room can manifest in a number of ways, including through feelings of rejection, lack of self-worth, lack of enthusiasm, rebellion, anger, promiscuity, lesbianism, addiction, and hard-heartedness, especially toward men. But God is a healer, and He has been releasing revelation into the earth to help women break free of past pain, rejection, feelings of abandonment, and other hurts that stem from a father wound. Books such as Bishop T. D. Jakes's *Woman, Thou Art Loosed* and *Daddy Loves His Girls*, Paula Sandford's *Healing for a Woman's Emotions*, and Joyce Meyer's *Beauty for Ashes* are excellent resources for discovering how to restore the years lost as a daughter and heal a woman's self-image.

If you're sensing that you that need deliverance in this room, pray the following:

> *Heavenly Father, I ask You to open the door to the room where You called me to be a daughter. I'm asking that You begin the process of my deliverance and restoration in this area.*
>
> *Holy Spirit, bring to light any demons dwelling in this room, and I command the demons of self-doubt, insecurity, and rejection, along with any generational curse of low self-esteem and spirits associated with a lack of identity as a daughter to come out of my emotions and be broken now in Jesus's name.*
>
> *Heavenly Father, I decree healing and restoration in the daughter room. I declare I have worth. I am Your daughter; You are my Father. My identity is found in You, and I will walk in the freedom of the daughter of the Most High God. In Jesus's name, amen.*

If you prayed that prayer, I would also encourage you to find a good church with a strong women's ministry to continue your healing in this area.

THE ETHNICITY ROOM

Before I close this chapter, I want to deal with one more room that both men and women share. It's a room that is often overlooked during deliverance ministry because our society encourages people to be proud of their nationality, race, and ethnicity. Though the Bible encourages us to walk in honor toward our family heritage, it's in this room that a mild form of racism can dwell, especially if you're a member of a race that has historically felt superior or inferior to other people groups.

Other demons connected to certain ethnic groups can also take up residence in this room. For instance, I've had tough sessions where it was hard to get Latino men delivered because their machismo wouldn't allow them to let go. So many times when conducting deliverance on those of Puerto Rican descent, I address the demons connected to the Taíno Indian tribe, and I have seen substantial results. Most have no idea that much of the resistance during deliverance is directly connected to issues related to their ethnicity.

Once while in Akron, Ohio, I was asked to minister to an elderly white woman who was suffering from demonic attacks of depression and mental health issues. As this lady's younger brother wheeled her into the office in a wheelchair, I was informed that she was a descendant of the man who coined the term "Jim Crow." The term started out as a stereotype of a black man in a nineteenth century song-and-dance act and eventually was used to describe any law that enforced racial segregation.[1]

This woman looked pitiful as she sat there saying, "I don't want to be free." Normally in cases where the person doesn't want freedom, I end the session. But in this case, after learning of her history, I immediately knew I was dealing with a demon attached to the fictitious Jim Crow her ancestor had created. I targeted the demon of racism and dismantled its power, and within ten minutes she went from saying she didn't want deliverance to asking me to pray for her because she wanted to be set free. Sometimes we have to be patient and persistent until the Holy Spirit breaks through and we can help the person get free.

Knowing the person's ethnicity can be critical for helping someone break generational curses that go way back in the bloodline. Generic prayers to break "any and all" generational curses aren't enough. You can't dismantle a curse you don't know exists. Family curses aren't just random dispositional behavior. Many times they're mental paradigms that are rooted in a person's upbringing and have been reinforced for years. It's possible that a good portion of the resistance you've faced in receiving deliverance is due to this area of race and ethnicity.

Demons of national pride, superiority and inferiority, racism, and cultural idolatry all have to be dealt with in a targeted manner. Once you order the demons in this room to leave, you will find that the person opens up more quickly, and they're much more willing to follow instructions leading to their freedom.

Use the following prayer to address demons that may be taking up residence in the ethnicity room:

> *Heavenly Father, You've made all nations to dwell on the earth, and You created them all equal. I'm grateful for the ethnic family You allowed me to be born into. I ask for forgiveness for being racially proud and indifferent toward those who are not like me. I renounce any forms of racism, racial indifference, and racial intolerance I have allowed in my life, whether knowingly or ignorantly. I command them to come out of the room in my life where my ethnicity resides in the name of Jesus. I dismantle any generational curses of racial pride now in Jesus's name. I release over my life love, unity, racial acceptance, reconciliation, and forgiveness in Jesus's name. May every part of my heart, mind, and soul view all ethnicities as equal. Amen.*

I've only scratched the surface here of the rooms that might need to be cleansed. There are ninety rooms in our temples, and I have addressed only a few here. As you seek the Holy Spirit for direction, He will show you which rooms, whether in your own life or someone else's, need to be cleansed. In closing this chapter, I want to share another story that shows the power of following the Holy Spirit's leading to discern which room needs to be cleansed.

One Saturday afternoon my wife and I were contacted by a minister asking if we would see a relative of his and help her go through deliverance, and we agreed to meet with her. This woman wasn't really going to church because she'd had a bad experience with the leadership of a particular congregation. We began to minister to her, but the session was dragging out, and it seemed we weren't getting anywhere. I had just caught the revelation of the rooms around that time, and I decided to test it since we were not having any breakthrough with traditional methods of deliverance.

Since she kept sharing how hurt she had been at church, I decided to use a different strategy. I sat in front of her and told her that I was going to sit in place of her pastor and ask for forgiveness. While sitting in front of her, I told her that I was going to enter the "Christian room," that part of her heart that loves the Lord's church and being around a community of believers. As soon as I sat down, the demons of "church hurt" began to manifest. I looked at her and said, "I'm sorry for hurting you as your pastor." Within minutes she was vomiting, weeping, screaming, and letting go of everything that was inside her. I've seen God bring incredible deliverance through the revelation of the rooms. If He has done it for others, He can do it for you!

CHAPTER 8

FOUR STEPS TO PURGE THE ROOMS

*When I arrived back in Jerusalem, I learned about
Eliashib's evil deed in providing Tobiah with a room
in the courtyards of the Temple of God. I became
very upset and threw all of Tobiah's belongings out of
the room. Then I demanded that the rooms be purified, and I brought back the articles for God's Temple.*
—NEHEMIAH 13:7–9

THERE ARE FAR more rooms in the soul than we have
discussed so far. After all, the temple Solomon built
had ninety rooms! The Holy Spirit is our teacher, and He
will guide us into all truth. If we ask Him to show us which
rooms have become areas of demonic habitation, He will.

As I have said many times, each person is different, and
though we all have some rooms in common, such as the ones
addressed in the previous chapter, be prepared for God to
reveal different rooms for different people. The good news is
that the same strategy works to cleanse every room. In the
Book of Nehemiah we find a foreshadowing of demons hiding in the rooms—and a four-step strategy to evict them.

Seventy years after King Nebuchadnezzar had lain waste
to Jerusalem during the Babylonian siege, King Cyrus of Persia allowed the Jews to return to the holy city to rebuild the

temple. (See Ezra 1:2–4.) Under the leadership of Zerubbabel the governor and Joshua the high priest, the exiles began this great work.

Years passed, and the rebuilding effort was taking longer than expected because the builders also had to guard the city, for the walls had been destroyed and the city was open to attack. Nehemiah, who was serving as a cupbearer to King Artaxerxes, heard about what was happening in Jerusalem and requested a leave of absence to rebuild the wall. His request was granted, and he and a group of Jews rebuilt the wall in fifty-two days (Neh. 6:15). Nehemiah united with Ezra the scribe, Zerubbabel the governor, and Joshua the high priest, and they established a type of apostolic structure in the city by assigning various leaders to serve in different capacities. Nehemiah then returned to Persia to serve King Artaxerxes.

After some time he was allowed to return to Jerusalem to check the work he had left in the charge of others. Upon returning, Nehemiah was made aware that Tobiah, an Ammonite official, had gained access to one of the rooms inside the temple. We're going to look closely at how Tobiah gained access to this room in the temple so you can see how the kingdom of darkness also gains access to the rooms in our temples.

Tobiah was a part of three family groups who returned to Jerusalem from exile and were claiming the rights of the priesthood. When the records were pulled, the lineage of the three families could not be verified, so they were banned from the priesthood. (See Ezra 2:59–60.) These families were also banned from eating the food allocated to the priests until the matter was taken before the Lord by inquiring of the Urim and Thummim (the sacred lots), which would provide a definitive answer. (See Ezra 2:63.)

The reason Tobiah couldn't be found in the registry of the priesthood is because he wasn't an Israelite. He was an Ammonite, a descendant of Abraham's nephew Lot and a distant relative of the nation of Israel. Because the Ammonites didn't help the children of Israel during their journey through the wilderness, God had said, "An Ammonite or Moabite shall not enter into the congregation of the LORD; even to their tenth generation shall they not enter into the congregation of the LORD forever" (Deut. 23:3, KJV). So the Law of Moses forbade them from entering the tabernacle.

In his anger Tobiah teamed up with a man named Sanballat and began a campaign to discourage Nehemiah from building the city walls. When they saw that their plan wasn't working, they looked for a way to legally enter the temple. Tobiah married the daughter of Shecaniah (Neh. 6:17–19), who was of the tribe of Judah, and found a way to get one of the grandsons of Eliashib the high priest to marry Sanballat's daughter (Neh. 13:28). Tobiah then used his connection to Eliashib to persuade him to give him access to the storerooms of the temple:

> Eliashib the priest, who had been appointed as supervisor of the storerooms of the Temple of our God and who was also a relative of Tobiah, had converted a large storage room and placed it at Tobiah's disposal. The room had previously been used for storing the grain offerings, the frankincense, various articles for the Temple, and the tithes of grain, new wine, and

olive oil (which were prescribed for the Levites, the singers, and the gatekeepers), as well as the offerings for the priests.

                                        —Nehemiah 13:4–5

Tobiah, who was an unauthorized priest, now had direct access to the temple rooms. What was once used to store the grain, frankincense, tithes, new wine, and oil for the temple worship was now at Tobiah's disposal.

The revelation of what was going on here is so clear. Demons have been prohibited from dwelling inside the human temple by the courtroom of heaven. The only loophole is if they are given permission to enter. This access is called a foothold, and this is why the apostle Paul warns us not to give place (a room) to the devil (Eph. 4:27). Once a person grants a demonic spirit access, it will enter as Tobiah did and begin removing the articles of the temple and replacing them with the accursed items.

If the demons can find legal ground to enter, they will. For example, the Bible says Ananias and Sapphira allowed Satan to fill their hearts when they chose to bring only part of the money from the sale of their property to the apostles but claimed they were giving all of it:

> Then Peter said, "Ananias, why have you let Satan fill your heart? You lied to the Holy Spirit, and you kept some of the money for yourself. The property was yours to sell or not sell, as you wished. And after selling it, the money was also yours to give away. How could you do a thing like this? You weren't lying to us but to God!"
>
>   —Acts 5:3–4

Was Ananias a true believer in the Lord? Yes! Did he give place to the devil? Yes.

Here's another example. Did the temple belong to Yahweh? Yes. But was one of its rooms under the control of Tobiah? Yes. In Ezekiel's vision of the temple in Ezekiel 43–44 was the temple filled with the glory of God? Yes. But were some of the rooms filled with idolatry and worship to false gods? Yes.

Let me again say here that not every problem is caused by a demon. But those who have been through counseling and inner healing with no breakthrough might need to consider that a demonic spirit may be involved. As the previous examples show, it is possible for the temple of the Lord to have evil spirits at work inside one of the rooms, and those demons need to be removed through targeted deliverance prayers.

Please hear me: I'm talking about prayers that are specific and detailed. Standing in front of a door yelling out generic prayers hoping the demons inside will leave won't get you far. No, we must stand before these rooms and use the keys of the kingdom to open the door, go inside, and cleanse the room. With our authority in Christ we can command the demons to leave and they have to obey.

This is what Nehemiah did. The Bible says that when he learned Tobiah had been given a room in the temple, he "became very upset and threw all of Tobiah's belongings out of the room. Then [he] demanded that the rooms be purified, and [he] brought back the articles for God's Temple, the grain offerings, and the frankincense" (Neh. 13:7–9).

This is a marvelous illustration of deliverance ministry.

Nehemiah gave us a guide for purging the rooms in the human temple and restoring them to their original purpose. It's a four-step process:

1. Recognize

2. Repudiate

3. Remove

4. Restore

For the remainder of this chapter we will look closely at each of these steps.

RECOGNIZE

The first step in the deliverance process is to *recognize* that these rooms in the human soul exist and that a believer can have a demon occupying them if the door is left open. The Greek word *ginōskō* is sometimes translated "recognize." It means "come to know" or "get a knowledge of."[1] The opposite of recognizing is denial, and denial is hard to overcome. Many believers today refuse to even acknowledge that demons are real and that a believer in Jesus can open a door that allows a demon to occupy a room in their hearts. Demons don't just hang out around open doors; as soon as they see an opportunity, they enter the rooms! The church of Jesus Christ's faulty theology and lack of discernment has kept countless believers with real demonic problems bound because you can't expel something you refuse to recognize.

This first step will require boldness and bravery because it may challenge what you've previously been taught to believe about demons. The apostle Paul says, "Examine yourselves to see if your faith is genuine. Test yourselves" (2 Cor. 13:5). This means we are to constantly perform self-diagnostics to make sure our beliefs line up with God's Word. When we do find something malfunctioning, we are to acknowledge and fix it, not deny that it's broken. In true biblical deliverance you acknowledge what's there and with the help of the Holy Spirit make the necessary adjustments to fix it.

The apostle Paul didn't deny his weaknesses; he actually acknowledged them when he said, "When I am weak, then I am strong" (2 Cor. 12:10). In the same chapter we also find him identifying the real problem, what he called "a messenger from Satan" (v. 7). The Greek word translated "messenger" in that verse is *aggelos*, which is also used to refer to angels. Paul was saying that this thorn in his flesh was actually a demon—an evil spirit sent on assignment to attack him. (But the chapter also reveals that God turned the situation around for Paul's good.) Paul was *not* saying he was possessed but rather that in one area of his body he was demonized (oppressed), as a thorn doesn't affect the whole body but punctures only one area.

Refusing to recognize the issue you're dealing with will result in continual malfunctioning in that area. Allow the Holy Spirit to bring light to your house. Allow Him to turn on the lights in dark rooms. Allow Him to go into areas in your heart that say "Do Not Enter" and acknowledge that you need the great Deliverer, Jesus Christ, to purge those rooms.

Nehemiah didn't hide himself when he discovered an intruder in the temple. He requested another leave of absence from serving King Artaxerxes so he could begin the process of restoration. Before Nehemiah returned to Jerusalem, he spent time fasting and praying, repenting before God, and confessing his sins and those of his ancestors. Confession is recognition. It's spending time before the Lord recognizing what's malfunctioning and petitioning Him, the manufacturer, to rebuild according to His original design.

You can use the following prayer prompt to invite the Holy Spirit to open your eyes and reveal any demons that may be operating in an area of your life or in the life of someone to whom you are ministering:

> Holy Spirit, I thank You for allowing me to sense the need for deliverance and cleansing in the rooms of my heart. I ask You to show me which rooms need to be cleansed. Show me which keys will open the doors. Grant me the boldness to open the door and turn on the lights. I ask You to reveal all the demons functioning in this room. [Be patient and let the Holy Spirit speak to you.]
>
> I thank You for guiding me into all truth and exposing the demon of _____ [name the demon the Holy Spirit shows you] so my deliverance process can begin. In Jesus's name, amen. [Continue praying as the Holy Spirit leads you.]

REPUDIATE

The second step is to *repudiate* the demons, which means "to refuse to have anything to do with"; "to refuse to accept"; "to reject as unauthorized"; "to refuse to acknowledge."[2] This step is just as important as the first. Demons are legalists; they must honor the legalities of the courtroom of heaven.

They can only carry out their function when humans violate the established edicts of heaven on earth. That is why when the prodigal son recognized his sin, the first thing he said was, "I have sinned against heaven" (Luke 15:21, KJV). In essence, he was saying he violated the commandments sanctioned by heaven's courtroom.

You must repudiate something verbally, not mentally, because demons don't read minds. The Bible says life and death are in the power of our tongues, not in the power of our thoughts. When Nehemiah returned to Jerusalem, he repudiated Tobiah publicly by refusing to acknowledge him anymore. I believe we must repudiate the work of the devil openly. Jesus said, "Everyone who acknowledges me publicly here on earth, I will also acknowledge before my Father in heaven. But everyone who denies me here on earth, I will also deny before my Father in heaven" (Matt. 10:32–33). You don't have to yell to be effective. I've had some people write down their renunciation of demonic spirits, and in group settings I've had others nod their heads to affirm that they renounce the devil's work in their lives. However it is done, the renunciation must be done openly.

When Nehemiah went to confront Tobiah and Eliashib, he didn't do it in secret; it was open and public for all to hear. Publicly repudiating Tobiah deactivated his authority over the room he occupied. If the repudiation had not been public, Nehemiah would have run the risk of being confronted by Tobiah's supporters or having his authority challenged for removing Tobiah from an area the high priest allowed him to use. To repudiate is to no longer acknowledge, and when the highest authorities of that time refused to acknowledge Tobiah, he had no choice but to cease his activity in the room.

The kingdom of darkness isn't obligated to obey our heart's desires or our thoughts. Demons respond to verbal directives when spoken with understanding and revelation. The demons that occupy these rooms know this and work hard to keep the believer from verbally renouncing them and their works. In the almost four hundred deliverance sessions I've led all over the world, the resistance remains the same. For the longest time, just when we reached the point in the session when the person seeking freedom is asked to verbally repudiate the demon and its work, the person would begin to feel like he was suffocating or like he was being choked. The person couldn't say "Jesus" or utter any other prayer.

In time I learned to command the demon to allow the person to speak and pray without interference. Then I'd lead him in the verbal confession. Once the person has verbally repudiated the demons, they have to leave. Demons know the rules and will obey, even if it doesn't look and feel as if they are responding to your commands. Trust that the courtroom of heaven has set the person's freedom in motion. If you as the deliverance worker or the person seeking freedom will proceed, there will be breakthrough.

Verbal repudiation is a targeted prayer directed at the demon you're renouncing. It is expressed with boldness as a directive, not an option. It's an affirmative use of one's authority that lets everyone know you cease to acknowledge something and are stripping it of all its rights and privileges. It also deactivates any voices of resistance, because once the demon is renounced, heaven responds immediately.

An example of this is found in Mark 5:7–8, when Jesus cast Legion out of the man in the Gerasenes:

> With a shriek, he screamed, "Why are you interfering with me, Jesus, Son of the Most High God? In the name of God, I beg you, don't torture me!" For Jesus had already said to the spirit, "Come out of the man, you evil spirit."

This passage is a clear example of repudiation. Jesus renounced the spirit. He didn't have to repeat Himself multiple times, as many charismatic believers who don't know any better do. Once is enough. Then by the power of the Holy Spirit, continue to enforce that declaration until every demon knows it has to go!

The following prayer prompt can be used to repudiate any demons that have been hiding in the rooms of your life or the life someone to whom you are ministering deliverance. However, before praying this prayer, read the entire chapter so you will know what steps to take after repudiating the demon. Like the other prayers in this book, this should be declared openly.

> *Satan and every demon hiding in the rooms of my heart, I renounce you. I disown you, and I cease to acknowledge your works. I command you demon of _____ [name the demon(s) the Holy Spirit shows you] to start preparing to leave my body in the name of Jesus. I no longer tolerate you or your works in my life. I repent and sever any legal contract that granted you authority to enter the room. By my authority in Christ, I remove all authority*

from every demon inside of me and declare them unauthorized. In the name of Jesus Christ, amen.

REMOVE

At this point the devil is screaming in terror because what frustrates unclean spirits most is being discovered. Demons are like roaches that work better in the dark and scurry when the lights are turned on. I would be surprised if you didn't feel some resistance as you follow the steps in this chapter. It's normal for you or the person receiving deliverance to feel distracted, suffocated, angry, foolish, or like it's not working; or to sweat or become nauseated. These are all normal signs that the demon is angry and putting up a last-ditch effort to stay in the room.

Whatever you do, don't stop now that its authority has been stripped. Now it's time to remove the demonic spirit. Demons won't leave simply because we desire for them go to. Nor do they read our minds. We must command them to leave in Jesus's name—and keep commanding them until they all leave.

This is where the confrontation begins. If you're helping someone receive freedom through deliverance, the demons will begin to display open forms of resistance. The manifestations include:

- Shrieking
- Animalistic movements
- Shouting insults
- Supernatural acts (I've seen demons throw people across the room, seen objects fall over

though no one touched them, heard male voices coming out of females, and seen one person's face take on the appearance of a gorilla.)

These are all designed to be like General Custer's last stand. They're trying to intimidate and scare you so they won't have to come out, but they have to leave. You can rest assured that though they are kicking and screaming, they are heading toward the exit.

Nehemiah took Tobiah's belongings, and with no fear or regret threw everything out of the room. That's what we must do. Use the following prompt to command the demons to leave. Again, this prayer should be declared openly.

> *I command every demon to leave my body now in the name of Jesus Christ. I open every door and window and order you to find an exit and leave. Leave me now and never return! Demon of _____ [name the demon(s) the Holy Spirit reveals to you], I order you by the courtroom of heaven to come out of the room now. Take your belongings with you and go back to the abyss where you came from, in Jesus's mighty name!*

RESTORE

After Nehemiah threw all Tobiah's belongings out of the room, he ordered that the room be purged and the articles of the temple that had been removed be returned.

> Then I demanded that the rooms be purified, and I
> brought back the articles for God's Temple, the grain
> offerings, and the frankincense.
>   —NEHEMIAH 13:9

When a demon is expelled, the room must be restored to its original purpose. This is done with your authority to bind and loose. You must release and restore what had been removed back into the room or empty area. So if the demon connected to unforgiveness was expelled, you must replace it with a fresh empowerment for forgiveness. If the demon of hate was removed, you must release the power of love to restore what the devil took. (If you don't know what to say, you can always declare blessing. Decreeing blessing is the same as declaring the opposite of what was removed.)

My favorite part of every deliverance session is watching the Holy Spirit restore joy, peace, gentleness, love, happiness, excitement, creativity, ideas, holiness, prayer, intimacy with God, and the like. It's actually the moment in deliverance ministry when you step back and watch the person bask in God's presence. The Holy Spirit and God's ministering angels are doing their sovereign work, and you get to be a fly on the wall to observe that holy moment. It's amazing!

Being able to witness divine restoration is an incredible privilege. It's why I do so much deliverance ministry. It brings tears to my eyes to watch the dark cloud veiling a person's features when he first begins the session dissipate so the individual's countenance shines with the glory of God. That is worth all the sacrifices that come with deliverance ministry.

The Greek word translated "restore" is *apokathistēmi*,

which can mean "to restore to its former state."[3] The ministry of deliverance is about manifesting the restoration of heaven in people's lives. We help restore them by removing the thief that stole their joy, peace, happiness, holiness, prayer life, marriage, ministry, etc. It's heaven's greatest pleasure to restore people. Restoration is their right as citizens of heaven.

This final step must also be done verbally, when you begin to function as a royal priest and declare the blessing of God upon your life or the person you just helped get free. It's done through what is called "commanded blessing," where you command God's blessing to be over, through, and upon the person. Without this process of restoration the deliverance is incomplete and you or the person receiving ministry run the risk of losing control again in this area. (You can receive deliverance as many times as you need until you're completely free.) The person is also vulnerable to becoming worse, as Jesus explained in Luke 11:24–26 (ESV):

> When the unclean spirit has gone out of a person, it passes through waterless places seeking rest, and finding none it says, "I will return to my house from which I came." And when it comes, it finds the house swept and put in order. Then it goes and brings seven other spirits more evil than itself, and they enter and dwell there. And the last state of that person is worse than the first.

Restoring what the enemy stole is vitally important. This is why you must function in your role as a royal priest and declare God's favor, blessing, glory, presence, etc. The Holy

Spirit wants to restore. It is the Father's will to restore. And nothing brings Jesus more pleasure than to restore what has been lost. We find Jesus restoring many things—sight to the blind, wholeness to the leper, life to the dead, and freedom to those who are bound. And He plans to give back to you what you've lost.

Use the following prompt to make a declaration for restoration:

> Thank You, Father, for my freedom and the cleansing of my rooms. I now declare with Your authority that I'm free and my rooms are cleansed. May Your glory sweep every room and put everything back in order. I order every door and window shut and sealed by the power of the name of Jesus. May the things taken from me be restored in my life now in Jesus's name.
>
> Holy Spirit, I thank You for this marvelous deliverance in Jesus's name.

If you've followed these four steps, you can rest in Christ, knowing your deliverance process has begun and heaven will respond. We have been promised in Scripture that whatever we bind and loose on earth will be bound and loosed in heaven. How marvelous it is to know that heaven is eager to join us in our freedom process. Hallelujah!

CHAPTER 9

PRAYERS FOR THE ROOMS AND BODY PARTS

He also tore down the living quarters of the male and female shrine prostitutes that were inside the Temple of the LORD, where the women wove coverings for the Asherah pole.

—2 KINGS 23:7

No OTHER PERSONALITY in the Bible was more zealous and determined to destroy any trace of idol worship and reestablish the true worship of Yahweh than King Josiah. His passionate, unwavering determination to eradicate the worship of false gods in Israel and in the temple makes him stand out among all the kings of Israel. God would be so impressed with this king's zeal that he was prophesied about three hundred years before he took the throne:

> At the LORD's command, a man of God from Judah went to Bethel....Then at the LORD's command, he shouted, "O altar, altar! This is what the LORD says: A child named Josiah will be born into the dynasty of David. On you he will sacrifice the priests from the pagan shrines who come here to burn incense, and human bones will be burned on you."

> —1 KINGS 13:1–2

King Josiah is an example of someone who will go to great lengths to break free from all demonic strongholds. The accounts of King Josiah's reign show one thing: he cleansed the temple of idolatry. Still today when someone leads a deliverance session, he is following in the footsteps of Josiah. God is raising up modern-day Josiahs who will dedicate themselves to dismantling the works of darkness in the temple and exposing the false priesthood plaguing the church. These Josiahs are living among us today.

If you're reading this book, I believe you're one of them! If it feels as if an ignition switch was turned on as you read this book, and you're someone who destroys any and all forms of unrighteousness in your life and others' and dismantles the works of darkness, *you're one of them*! The revelation in this book has been sanctioned and released to a remnant of believers who will carry the mantle of Josiah.

Read the following passage through the lens of deliverance and see the targeted zeal Josiah had for bringing reform. Deliverance must be targeted in order for it to be effective. Josiah's reform in the land of Israel and the temple was a strategic effort. And it was a prototype for the ministry of deliverance today.

> Then the king instructed Hilkiah the high priest and the priests of the second rank and the Temple gate-keepers to remove from the LORD's Temple all the articles that were used to worship Baal, Asherah, and all the powers of the heavens. The king had all these things burned outside Jerusalem on the terraces of the Kidron Valley, and he carried the ashes away to Bethel. He did away with the idolatrous priests, who

> had been appointed by the previous kings of Judah,
> for they had offered sacrifices at the pagan shrines
> throughout Judah and even in the vicinity of Jerusa-
> lem. They had also offered sacrifices to Baal, and to
> the sun, the moon, the constellations, and to all the
> powers of the heavens. The king removed the Ash-
> erah pole from the LORD's Temple and took it out-
> side Jerusalem to the Kidron Valley, where he burned
> it. Then he ground the ashes of the pole to dust and
> threw the dust over the graves of the people. He also
> tore down the living quarters of the male and female
> shrine prostitutes that were inside the Temple of the
> LORD, where the women wove coverings for the Ash-
> erah pole.
>
> —2 KINGS 23:4–7

This passage reveals only a portion of the amazing things
Josiah did to bring reform. It also shows just how steeped
in idolatry the children of Israel were. No other chapter in
the Bible exposes this many idols within the temple, some
of which had been there as long as the reign of the northern
kingdom's first king, Jeroboam.

CLEANSING OUR TEMPLES

That is our call today—to cleanse our temples and to help
others get free. I want to close this chapter with the following list of additional parts of the body that can become a
habitation for demons. It is my mission to see people walk in
complete freedom, so as God gives me revelation into body
parts where the enemy hides, I share it with others.

With each body part I have included a relevant scripture and a prayer written to be used for self-deliverance, but

deliverance ministers can adapt them for their purposes. In many of these body parts the demonic activity will manifest as sickness. But when applicable, I include other manifestations of demonic activity in those areas.

I am amazed at the results I have seen since God began giving me this revelation of demons hiding in the rooms of our souls and our body parts, but I know there is so much more for the body of Christ to discover. Be open to hearing the Holy Spirit speak to you about parts of the body not included in this chapter so you can continue to go deeper in deliverance!

The blood

> For the life of the body is in its blood. I have given you the blood on the altar to purify you, making you right with the LORD.
> —LEVITICUS 17:11

Decree freedom in this part of the body by saying this prayer out loud:

> *Lord Jesus, may Your precious blood purge and sanctify my blood. May all demonic contamination leave my blood. May all diseases assigned to the blood be eradicated from my system now in Jesus's name. I order every demon hiding within my bloodline to be severed and removed. I break every ungodly blood covenant made in my bloodline now in the name of Jesus. May the Holy Spirit create new blood cells within my blood type now in Jesus's name. Amen.* [Continue praying as the Holy Spirit guides you.]

The breasts

> Aaron then lifted up the breasts and right thighs as a special offering to the LORD, just as Moses had commanded.
>
> —LEVITICUS 9:21

Decree freedom in this body part by saying this prayer out loud:

> *Heavenly Father, I decree that all forms of malfunction and diseases in my breasts must begin to regulate now in the name of Jesus! All demons hiding in the chest must be removed now. Holy Spirit, place Your finger on my chest area and cause anything unauthorized to be resolved. In Jesus's name, amen.* [Continue praying as the Holy Spirit guides you.]

The fat

> And he shall take off from it all the fat of the bullock for the sin offering; the fat that covered the inwards, and all the fat that is upon the inwards.
>
> —LEVITICUS 4:8, KJV

Decree freedom in this part of the body by saying this prayer out loud:

> *Father, in the name of Jesus, I declare that every part of my body that is contaminated with that which doesn't glorify You be removed now. May the healing virtue that rested upon Jesus without measure come upon me now in Jesus's name. I speak to*

the muscle tissue in my body and command it to regulate and be free of every demon! I decree this in the name of Jesus. Amen. [Continue praying as the Holy Spirit guides you.]

The hands

They came to Moses and Aaron that day and said, "We have become ceremonially unclean by touching a dead body. But why should we be prevented from presenting the LORD's offering at the proper time with the rest of the Israelites?"

—NUMBERS 9:6–7

Decree freedom in this body part by saying this prayer out loud:

Father in heaven, I ask You to forgive me for touching the unclean thing. I ask that You wash me in the blood of Jesus and sanctify my sense of touch. May every cell in my body assigned to touching be cleansed now in Jesus's name. I command every demon to leave every part of my body that is connected to touching. Holy Spirit, touch me now in Jesus's name. Amen. [Continue praying as the Holy Spirit guides you.]

The hips

See now his strength is in his hips, and his power is in the muscles of his belly.   —JOB 40:16, MEV

Decree freedom in this body part by saying this prayer out loud:

> *Every demon hiding in my hip bones, every demon causing waist discomfort, every unclean spirit causing hip dysfunction and pain, I command all of you to release my hips now in the name of Jesus. Heavenly Father, touch my hips and cause supernatural healing. I will walk straight. I will run for Your glory. I will bend my hips like normal. In the name of Christ Jesus, amen.* [Continue praying as the Holy Spirit guides you.]

The joints

> For the word of God is quick, and powerful, and sharper than any twoedged sword, piercing even to the dividing asunder of soul and spirit, and of the joints and marrow, and is a discerner of the thoughts and intents of the heart.
>
> —HEBREWS 4:12, KJV

Decree freedom in this part of the body by saying this prayer out loud:

> *Lord, all my joints belong to You. You have fitly placed my joints together. May Your anointing allow my joints to connect according to Your perfect design. May they have oil from Your presence between them and function at full capacity. I command every demon living in my joints to come out of me now in Jesus's name. Spirits of infirmity, release your hold on my joints. Spirit of God, regulate all*

the hinges and joints in my body now in Jesus's name
so I can run and leap before Your presence. Amen.
[Continue praying as the Holy Spirit guides you.]

The knees

Wherefore lift up the hands which hang down, and
the feeble knees.
                                    —HEBREWS 12:12, KJV

In addition to physical illness, signs of demons hiding
in this part of the body include fear, prayerlessness, and an
inability to stand on one's own. Decree freedom in this body
part by saying this prayer out loud:

I command my knees and legs to be in perfect health
now in the name of Jesus. I order every demon caus-
ing knee problems to leave my body now in Jesus's
name. All demons causing my knees discomfort so I
won't pray, I order you to come out now. Holy Spirit,
let the same power that allowed Jesus to pray on His
knees and to walk tirelessly preaching the kingdom
be upon me now in Jesus's name. Amen. [Continue
praying as the Holy Spirit guides you.]

The lungs

You let the world, which doesn't know the first thing
about living, tell you how to live. You filled your lungs
with polluted unbelief, and then exhaled disobedience.
                                    —EPHESIANS 2:2, THE MESSAGE

Decree freedom in this body part by saying this prayer
out loud:

Father, in the name of Jesus, I decree that right now as I inhale, Your glory fills my lungs and saturates every part of my respiratory system with Your presence, causing me to be filled with life, power, glory, and strength. As I exhale, I command every demon hiding in my lungs to come out! In Jesus's name, amen. [Take a couple breaths, and exhale every demon and inhale the presence of God. Continue praying as the Holy Spirit leads.]

The neck

For I know thy rebellion, and thy stiff neck: behold, while I am yet alive with you this day, ye have been rebellious against the LORD; and how much more after my death?

—DEUTERONOMY 31:27, KJV

In addition to physical illness, signs of demons hiding in this part of the body include rebellion, stubbornness, being unteachable, and being stuck in one's old ways. Decree freedom in this body part by saying this prayer out loud:

Father, in the name of Jesus, my neck belongs to You, and You adorned it with precious chains of truth and righteousness. I carry Your commandments around my neck and close to my heart. I command any demon living within my neck and causing me pain and discomfort to come out now in Jesus's name. All demons of rebellion, leave my neck area now! Holy Spirit, let Your power heal every muscle, tissue, and nerve, and heal all neck injuries in the name of Jesus. Amen. [Continue praying as the Holy Spirit guides you.]

The seed

As arrows are in the hand of a mighty man; so are children of the youth. Happy is the man that hath his quiver full of them: they shall not be ashamed, but they shall speak with the enemies in the gate.

—PSALM 127:4–5, KJV

Decree freedom in this part of the body by saying this prayer out loud:

I order every demon hiding within my body and keeping me from being fruitful to leave right now in Jesus's name. Father, may the virtue of Abraham that caused him to have a child in his old age be upon me now in Jesus's name. Let my body function as You intended. Amen. [Continue praying as the Holy Spirit guides you.]

The shoulders

As I have planned, so shall it be, and as I have purposed, so shall it stand, that I will break the Assyrian in my land, and on my mountains trample him underfoot; and his yoke shall depart from them, and his burden from their shoulder.

—ISAIAH 14:24–25, ESV

Decree freedom in this body part by saying this prayer out loud:

> Lord Jesus, Your Word says the government of the world has been placed upon Your shoulders. Lord, You transferred that same authority to me. Jesus, You said that Your yoke is easy and Your burden is light (Matt. 11:30). I decree that Your burden upon my shoulder would be easy and that every spirit of heaviness in my shoulders must leave now in Jesus's name. May the weight of Your glory come upon my shoulders now in Jesus's name. Amen. [Continue praying as the Holy Spirit guides you.]

The sinews (an archaic term for nerves)

> My bones are pierced in me in the night season: and my sinews take no rest.
>
> —JOB 30:17, KJV

Decree freedom in this part of the body by saying this prayer out loud:

> Heavenly Father, I ask that You heal all the nerves in my body. Every demon hiding in any nerve in my flesh, come out now. Holy Spirit, breathe on my nervous system and cause all irregularities to be healed and function according to God's original design. In Jesus's name, amen. [Continue praying as the Holy Spirit guides you.]

The skeleton

> My frame was not hidden from thee, when I was made in secret, and curiously wrought in the lowest parts of the earth.
>
> —PSALM 139:15, ASV

Decree freedom in this part of the body by saying this prayer out loud:

> Heavenly Father, every bone in my body belongs to You. Your plan, purposes, and power are hidden within my bones. My bones are anointed, and I command every demon to leave my bones now in Jesus's name. I decree healing in the marrow of my bones. I declare that my every bone is healthy. Holy Spirit, let Your presence rest upon my skeletal system in Jesus's name! Amen. [Continue praying as the Holy Spirit guides you.]

The stomach

> The words of a talebearer are as wounds, and they go down into the innermost parts of the belly.
> —PROVERBS 18:8, KJV

Decree freedom in this body part by saying this prayer out loud:

> Jesus, You said that rivers of living water would flow out of my belly. I decree that the rivers of almighty God flood every part of my belly now in Jesus's name. May the rivers of the Holy Spirit carry away every demon lurking or hiding within my belly now in Jesus's name. I declare the virtue of the Holy Spirit is healing all stomach diseases and intestinal issues. May my belly be open to receive the scrolls and deposits of heaven. In Jesus's name, amen. [Continue praying as the Holy Spirit guides you.]

The tissue

> Then as I watched, muscles and flesh formed over the bones. Then skin formed to cover their bodies, but they still had no breath in them.
>
> —EZEKIEL 37:8

Decree freedom in this part of the body by saying this prayer out loud:

> *I decree that every tissue in my body must be purged by the blood of Jesus and regenerated by the power of the Holy Spirit. I command every demon to leave my tissues now in Jesus's name. I command my tissues to be made new like the tissues the prophet Ezekiel saw in the valley of dry bones. I call this forth now in Jesus's name. Amen.* [Continue praying as the Holy Spirit guides you.]

The unpresentable parts

> And on those parts of the body that we think less honorable we bestow the greater honor, and our unpresentable parts are treated with greater modesty.
>
> —1 CORINTHIANS 12:23, ESV

Decree freedom in these parts of the body by saying this prayer out loud:

> *Father, in the name of Jesus, I ask that the Holy Spirit touch every part of my body that is not easily visible or discussed frequently. Spirit of God, I ask You to search within my body and find every demon concealed in any body part or any area of my spirit*

*and remove it. Every demon hiding in the uncomely
parts, I renounce you and order you out of my body.
May the glory of the Lord rest upon my body like the
waters cover the sea. In Jesus's name, amen.* [Continue praying as the Holy Spirit guides you.]

PRAYER AGAINST DEMONS HIDING IN THE ROOMS

Use the following prayer to evict any demons hiding in the rooms of your life. Ask the Holy Spirit to show you what room needs to be addressed and use the guides in chapter 8 to remove every demon associated with that room. Remember, be patient and wait for the Holy Spirit to speak. Address every demonic spirit He reveals to you so that room will be completely cleansed.

> *I command every demon of _____ hiding
> in the _____ room, to come out in Jesus's
> name, and I decree _____
> _____. In Jesus's name!*

After going through this level of deliverance, you can rest assured that the house is swept clean and put in order. You're now ready to walk in the abundance Jesus promised, for the contamination that was keeping you from walking in the fullness of your purpose and calling has been removed. You are now free to utilize the keys of the kingdom to open the rooms that had previously been closed and experience intimacy with the Holy Spirit like never before. As Jesus declared, "If the Son sets you free, you are truly free" (John 8:36).

NOTES

CHAPTER 1
THE MYSTERY OF PROTOTYPE TIMING

1. *Merriam-Webster*, s.v. "prototype," accessed January 19, 2018, https://www.merriam-webster.com/dictionary/prototype.

2. Blue Letter Bible, s.v. *"mishkan,"* accessed January 19, 2018, https://www.blueletterbible.org/lang/Lexicon/Lexicon.cfm?strongs=H4908&t=KJV.

CHAPTER 2
THE BLUEPRINT OF THE TEMPLE

1. Christian Kumpost, "The Right Question (I, Robot)," YouTube video, posted August 21, 2017, https://www.youtube.com/watch?v=ZKxr0wyIic4.

2. Blue Letter Bible, s.v. *"ophthalmos,"* accessed January 22, 2018, https://www.blueletterbible.org/lang/Lexicon/Lexicon.cfm?strongs=G3788&t=KJV.

3. See images of Solomon's temple at StopAndPrayTV, accessed February 22, 2018, https://stopandpraytv.wordpress.com/2015/06/08/in-the-ancient-near-east-kingship-and-temple-building-went-hand-in-hand/; Lambert Dolphin, "The Temple of Solomon," accessed February 22, 2018, http://www.templemount.org/solomon.html; and Nancy Missler, "The Temple of God—'The Hidden Part,'" Koinonia House, October 1, 1997, http://www.khouse.org/articles/1997/273/

CHAPTER 3
UNDERSTANDING THE
REGULATIONS AND PROCEDURES

1. Blue Letter Bible, s.v. *"chuqqah,"* accessed January 22, 2018, https://www.blueletterbible.org/lang/Lexicon/Lexicon.cfm ?strongs=H2708&t=KJV.

2. Blue Letter Bible, s.v. *"choq,"* accessed January 22, 2018, https://www.blueletterbible.org/lang/Lexicon/lexicon.cfm?page =2&strongs=H2706&t=KJV.

3. *Merriam-Webster,* s.v. "regulation," accessed January 22, 2018, https://www.merriam-webster.com/dictionary/regulations.

4. Blue Letter Bible, s.v. *"kanōn,"* accessed January 22, 2018, https://www.blueletterbible.org/lang/Lexicon/Lexicon.cfm ?strongs=G2583&t=KJV.

5. *Merriam-Webster,* s.v. "procedure," accessed January 22, 2018, https://www.merriam-webster.com/dictionary/procedure.

CHAPTER 4
IDENTIFYING DEMONIC ENTRANCES AND EXITS

1. The *Targum Onkelos,* a respected Aramaic translation of the Torah, defines "living being" (referenced in Genesis 2:7 in relation to Adam) as a "speaking spirit." For more, see "March 2008," Billye Brim Ministries, accessed November 13, 2017, https://www.billyebrim.org/content/march_2008.

2. Charles Spence, "Just How Much of What We Taste Derives From the Sense of Smell?," Abstract, *Flavour* (November 2, 2015), https://flavourjournal.biomedcentral.com/articles /10.1186/s13411-015-0040-2.

3. Blue Letter Bible, s.v. *"pneuma,"* accessed January 22, 2018, https://www.blueletterbible.org/lang/Lexicon/Lexicon.cfm ?strongs=G4151&t=KJV.